A PLUME BOOK

BEFORE YOU BUY!

MICHAEL CORBETT is the Real Estate and Lifestyle correspondent of NBC's number-one-rated nationally syndicated news magazine *Extra*. Utilizing his expertise in real estate, home, and lifestyle, Corbett also hosts and produces NBC's *Extra's Mansions & Millionaires!*, *Extra*'s top-rated weekend show, with over 2.4 million viewers per week.

An accomplished bestselling author, Corbett shares his real estate expertise with his first two top-selling books, *Find It, Fix It, Flip It! Make Millions in Real Estate—One House at a Time* and *Ready, Set, Sold! The Insider Secrets to Sell Your House Fast—for Top Dollar!* In these books, he shares the strategies, tips, and never-before-revealed insider techniques that have helped him make a fortune in real estate.

His years of experience in buying, renovating, and selling homes have made him a sought-after real estate expert. Corbett is a go-to real estate expert, with regular appearances on *Larry King Live* and featured regularly on the Discovery Channel, HGTV, *LIVE! with Regis and Kelly*, CNN, ABC News, Fox News, the Fine Living Network, *The Tyra Banks Show*, *Good Day Live*, and CBS News, and in *People* magazine, *Newsweek*, *Robb Report*, the *Los Angeles Times*, and the *New York Times*. He also hosted and lectured on the Real Estate & Wealth Expo's twelve-city national tour, sharing the stage with Donald Trump, Tony Robbins, Suze Orman, Robert Kiyosaki, and Dr. Alan Greenspan to crowds of five to ten thousand people.

In addition to his hosting, producing, writing, and real estate talents, Corbett has certainly made his mark in daytime television. He was voted "Daytime's Most Lovable Cad" by *People* magazine, for his red-hot starring roles in three different soap operas. He first starred for three years on *Ryan's Hope* for ABC, next for four years on *Search for Tomorrow* for NBC, and then nine years playing David Kimball on the CBS number-one daytime ratings grabber in the United States, Canada, and Europe, *The Young and the Restless*.

Corbett, a true real estate entrepreneur, has been buying, renovating, and selling homes for over twenty-five years. His company, Highland Properties, which he founded at the age of twenty-one, has bought, restored, and sold dozens of homes and apartment buildings.

For more information, visit his Web site at www.MichaelCorbett .com.

PLUME
Published by the Penguin Group
Penguin Group (USA) Inc., 375 Hudson Street, New York, New York 10014, U.S.A.
Penguin Group (Canada), 90 Eglinton Avenue East, Suite 700, Toronto, Ontario, Canada M4P
2Y3 (a division of Pearson Penguin Canada Inc.) • Penguin Books Ltd., 80 Strand, London
WC2R 0RL, England • Penguin Ireland, 25 St. Stephen's Green, Dublin 2, Ireland (a division
of Penguin Books Ltd.) • Penguin Group (Australia), 250 Camberwell Road, Camberwell,
Victoria 3124, Australia (a division of Pearson Australia Group Pty. Ltd.) • Penguin Books
India Pvt. Ltd., 11 Community Centre, Panchsheel Park, New Delhi – 110 017, India • Pen-
guin Group (NZ), 67 Apollo Drive, Rosedale, North Shore 0632, New Zealand (a division of
Pearson New Zealand Ltd.) • Penguin Books (South Africa) (Pty.) Ltd., 24 Sturdee Avenue,
Rosebank, Johannesburg 2196, South Africa

Penguin Books Ltd., Registered Offices: 80 Strand, London WC2R 0RL, England

First published by Plume, a member of Penguin Group (USA) Inc.

First Printing, March 2011
10   9   8   7   6   5   4   3   2   1

ILLUSTRATION CREDITS: Illustrations on pages 8, 79, 80, 81, 83, 121, 122, 126, 129, 204, 205, 210,
226, 243, 260 by Mindi Meader. Illustrations on pages 1, 25, 71, 153, 193 by Steve Moore.
Chart on pages 199–202, copyright 2009 Closing.com. All photos from the collection of the
author.

 REGISTERED TRADEMARK—MARCA REGISTRADA

ISBN 978-0-452-29680-0
CIP data is available.

Printed in the United States of America
Set in Bembo Lt Std • Designed by Eve L. Kirch

BEFORE YOU BUY!

The Homebuyer's Handbook
for Today's Market

MICHAEL CORBETT

A PLUME BOOK

I dedicate this book to two very dear friends who left us this past year. They both taught me so much about real estate, renovation, design . . . and life. I would not be the person I am today were it not for their powerful gifts. They are so very missed.
For you, Brian Hatch and Steven Wilder.

Contents

Part Two: Preparing to Buy

Part Three: Smart Shopping

Part Five: Closing

Foreword

It seems like it was just yesterday when I sold my first home as a real estate agent, even though it was way back in 1975. I had majored in parks and recreation at the University of Illinois and prepared for a career working with youth. I coached and taught math before getting what I thought was my dream job as youth program director at the YMCA in La Grange, Illinois. I loved working with the kids, enjoyed helping them learn, and valued being a member of the Y family. My friend and tennis partner Jack Lidbetter, who managed a Gallery of Homes real estate office in La Grange, told me on several occasions that I would be great in real estate, but he really got me when he said I could still help people while making more money as an agent. After months of discussions with him, I agreed, left the Y, and went into real estate full-time.

I went to all of the people I knew and told them I was now a real estate agent. One of those I spoke with was the secretary at the Y. She and her husband had always wanted to own a home, but they didn't make a lot of money and figured it would never happen. They were resigned to renting. But when we sat down and ran the numbers—essentially a rent vs. buy comparison—they were surprised to learn they could afford a home! I helped get them an FHA loan and they eventually zeroed in on a small starter home. Believe me, it was not opulent but to them it was the Taj Mahal.

I remember taking them over to the home for one final look. Afterward they returned to my car while I went in and negotiated with the seller's agent. I was successful with the negotiation and I could not wait to share the news with them. I coolly walked to my car and almost screamed, "Congratulations! You are now homeowners!" It was an emotional moment and we all cried. I even gave up my commission to help them with the down payment. That was 1975, but I remember it like it was just yesterday.

Jack was right. I could help people and make a difference. I was hooked. Thankfully I have gone on to spend all but one of my thirty-six years in real estate with the Coldwell Banker brand, the last six years as CEO.

All through my career I have often returned to that first sale because it was indicative of what homeownership means. We don't aspire to rent. We aspire to own. Homeownership is part of the American Dream and always will be.

I remember when my parents bought our first house. We had lived on my grandparents' farm in southern Illinois until my parents bought a home in the suburbs of Chicago. It was a lifestyle decision and a big investment. But my parents did not look at our house as a piggy bank. Like most in their generation, they did not look at their home as an easy way to get rich. The phrase "home appreciation" was rarely—if ever—uttered. Instead, they viewed our house as a place of our own and a place for my sister, Mary, and me to grow up.

But times have changed. Back in the mid-2000s, we were at the tail end of one of the greatest housing booms of all time. Homeownership rates rose and median home prices jumped by nearly 50 percent from a decade prior, to $221,900 in 2006. Many of us became obsessed with how much our homes appreciated in value, and online property value estimators like ours at www.ColdwellBanker.com gained enormous popularity. We saw speculators, real estate investors, and the era of "McMansions." Unfortunately greed took over. Too many people, encouraged by low teaser rates offered by unscrupulous mortgage lenders, bought homes they couldn't really afford.

So when the market, which at that point I continually referred to as "unsustainable" in countless interviews, slowed down, most thought home prices would level off, as they have done historically after a sustained strong period. But they didn't. They went down. The National

Association of Realtors (NAR) reported that national median prices in 2007 had dropped from the previous year—for the first time since World War II. Because of the catastrophic impact of subprime loans, coupled with the horrible greed seen on Wall Street, foreclosures became a huge drag on the market and housing became a key cause of the Great Recession of 2008.

The first decade of this century was fascinating. The highs of the housing boom were followed by the lowest of lows. So what remains is a confused, nervous, and reluctant potential homeowner. Let's face it. Even during the best of times, buying a home is an arduous process. This is especially true for first-timers. There is a natural uneasiness as terms like "down payment," "preapproval," "mortgage rates," "home inspection," "closing," and others pop up on a daily basis. There is also the pressure to find the right real estate agent. Throw in the market conditions, and a median home price decline to a 2003 level of approximately $173,000, and there is even greater cause for buyer concern.

But through it all, people buy and sell homes for lifestyle reasons. Homeownership is part of the circle of life. Babies, marriages, job transfers, promotions, and even the sadder parts of life like divorce, prolonged job loss, catastrophic illness, and death.

But it is also important to remember that homeownership is not for everyone. It is a deeply personal decision. Are you comfortable with the financial responsibility of homeownership? Do you want to be responsible for maintenance and upkeep? Are you at the right phase of your life? How long do you plan to stay in the home? There are so many questions to answer.

So even through the recession, many are still buying a home. While more than 7 million homes were sold nationally in 2005, today we are back in the 5 million range, up about 55 percent from twenty years ago. That is still a lot of home sales. And for those who have the lifestyle need, the desire to own a home, and the financial viability and job stability necessary, now is the smartest time to buy a home in the thirty-six years I have been in real estate.

The perception of homeownership is changing. No longer are we looking at our homes as the key to great wealth; instead we are looking at our homes as an investment in our lifestyle.

I am not suggesting that we do not want to make money when

we sell a home. As we return to more normalized market conditions, we will likely see historical annual gains on our homes. And that is fine. So while I doubt we can, or should, go back to the days of my parents and put the genie back in the bottle about the financial benefits of homeownership, at least we can become a bit more realistic.

—Jim Gillespie, CEO, Coldwell Banker Real Estate

Acknowledgments

Having now written three books, I have realized that I want to acknowledge both the people directly responsible for their contributions to this book and also those who are part of the fabric of my life as well.

I first want to sincerely thank everyone at Plume. They have been my champions from the day I signed the deal for my first book with them. Thank you Clare Ferraro, Cherise Fisher, Kate Napolitano, and Mary Pompano.

My literary agent, Bonnie Solow, with her roster of illustrious bestselling authors, has been such a wonderful mentor. I often think back to my very first meeting with her at the Newsroom Café in Los Angeles. She possesses the amazing combination of vision, wisdom, and practical advice. My editor Kristin Loberg is a wonderful writer in her own right, who has the uncanny ability to find a solution to any problem.

David Siroty at Coldwell Banker Real Estate, whom I have grown to both enjoy and respect. Mindi Meader, a gifted artist and illustrator, has such a talent for designing my charts and graphs. I also want to thank my manager, Milt Suchin, and of course my executive producer at *Extra*, Lisa Gregorisch-Dempsey.

That brings me to the rest of my life and the people who are the constants in my life today. They are Cheryl O'Neil, James Pelk, and

Warren Coulter. Also on that list is of course my mom, who continues to champion and encourage me daily.

And last, my father. He loved to read and loved books. If he were still alive, I know he would have copies of my books sitting on his desk, dog-eared and worn from reading and rereading.

Introduction

I always save the introduction for last when writing a book. Seriously, it is always the hardest thing for me to write. Especially this time around.

Here is my dilemma: This is my third book, following *Find It, Fix It, Flip It! Make Millions in Real Estate—One House at a Time* and *Ready, Set, Sold! The Insider Secrets to Sell Your House Fast—for Top Dollar!* So the problem is, with two other books already written, I've penned two other introductions. In those introductions, I talked all about my love of real estate, how I began buying and fixing up homes, how I joyously juggle a very successful acting and television career, and how I became a bestselling real estate author and national expert on the subject. So, if you read my first two books, you know all this! But if you haven't, then I suppose I have to tell you the story as succinctly and as interestingly as possible.

I won't be offended if you jump ahead two pages. But if you haven't read my previous books, then read these next couple pages and you'll get to know a little bit about me, my career on television, and, most important, why I have become such an avid spokesman for and supporter of homebuyers and homeowners. I have become a voice for the consumer, because I am a consumer, homebuyer, and homeowner just like you.

How I Got Started

I have been buying properties for over twenty-five years. I purchased my first home when I was nineteen years old. I had no idea what I was doing and I was terrified. I knew nothing about real estate, buying, or selling, and, like any novice, I did everything wrong. I was just out of college and venturing into acting. I had just landed my first big job, a three-year contract on the ABC daytime soap opera *Ryan's Hope*.

After about six months on the show, I received my first bonus check. It was for $10,000 and I thought I was the richest and luckiest guy on the planet. I knew I should invest it immediately. But how? While spending some time with my family one weekend, I noticed that the house next to my grandmother's in Collingswood, New Jersey, had a For Sale sign on the front lawn. I called the number on the sign and said, "Hi, I want to buy the house on Coulter Avenue." The Realtor responded, "Meet me there in fifteen minutes." I told the Realtor that my grandmother lived next door and I wanted the house. I offered full price. I didn't know how to negotiate and I had no Realtor representing me. I didn't even know to ask for an inspection or any contingencies.

Well, obviously I overpaid and my purchase process was primed for disaster. But by sheer luck and good instincts I bungled through the deal and the closing. I fixed the house up and then brought in some furniture from my grandmother's garage to make it look nice for potential buyers. I put it back on the market, sold it right away, and, thankfully, to my amazement, made some pretty good money on the deal. Hmmm, I knew I was onto something.

I look back and realize that if I had known then what I know now about real estate, I would have paid less, saved on expenses, and made much more money. I wish I had read a book like this one, back when I bought that first house.

Many Years Later

At last count, I have bought, fixed, renovated, rented, or sold more than thirty-five houses and rental properties—in both good markets and bad markets. During my entire seventeen years on daytime television, including a three-year run on *Ryan's Hope*, five years on *Search for Tomorrow*, and a nine-year stint on *The Young and the Restless*, I was fixing up and selling houses and buying rental properties on the side. Over the past ten years, I have had the great fortune to combine both my career in television and my love of real estate as the real estate and lifestyle host of NBC's *Extra* and host and senior producer of *Extra's Mansions & Millionaires*. I am also now a regular featured expert and guest on *Larry King Live*, CNN, HGTV, the Fine Living Network, and the TLC Network, and a source of real estate info for reporters at the *New York Times*, *Forbes*, *Smart Money*, the *Los Angeles Times*, and the *Miami Herald*.

What Inspired Me to Write This Book

Today the real estate market is crazy. No one is sure *what* to do or *how* to do it.

Homebuyers are standing on the sidelines in frustration and confusion.

So many homebuyers have made so many mistakes. So many jumped in blindly to homeownership without having the facts and the real information. Many homebuyers made critical missteps and decisions when buying. Homebuyers overpaid, overspent, and bought homes they could not afford. They fell prey to the hype and the misinformation. It makes me very sad to see that. Because a huge percentage of the home-buying and home-owning problem could have been avoided had those homeowners been educated.

I don't want to see any more homebuyers make those same mistakes. I have always been extremely conservative when it comes to real estate. My approach is to make low-risk, practical, and safe choices. I would always rather a homebuyer miss out on the house of his dreams than find himself locked into a house he can't afford. I have been teaching "safe and sane" for years. Now more than ever, after this massive real estate and economic fallout, it is imperative to know how to buy safe, sane, and smart. That is why it was so important for me to write this book.

Why You Need This Book, in This Market, Now

The thought of jumping into homeownership today can be terrifying. Buying the wrong house at the wrong price with the wrong mortgage could spell financial disaster for you and your family. One mistake can result in thousands of dollars in unnecessary higher costs, fees, expenses, and bottom-line prices. The difference between home-buying success and failure in today's market is having the information and advice needed to make smart decisions and choices.

I have written *Before You Buy!* to be a road map for all future homebuyers. It gives you the no-nonsense, hype-free, and practical information to Buy Safe, Buy Sane, and Buy Smart! It presents information, tools, proven methods, expert advice, and insights from top real estate professionals.

In fact, one of the most knowledgeable names in real estate today is Jim Gillespie, CEO of Coldwell Banker Real Estate. I was fortunate enough to first meet Jim when he offered the cover endorsement for one of my previous books. I have wanted to work more with him ever since. So for this book, I am thrilled to have access to his knowledge and expertise. And I am very excited that he is not only writing the foreword for this book but also is contributing some fantastic information throughout the book.

A buyer who learns from the pros and utilizes their expertise is an educated, empowered buyer who secures the best deal, the most advantageous mortgage, and the right home for his budget. These are the buyers who will make their purchasing dollars go further— allowing them to buy *more* house for *less* money. And that means buying a house that is actually affordable!

I have been insisting to all my friends that before they even think about buying right now . . . they read this book! Today's market is the perfect time to get more house for your money . . . at a price you can afford—if you know how to do it. So, as I tell all my coworkers, students, and friends, Before You Buy . . . read on!

PART ONE

Why Buy, Why Now, and Why You!

CHAPTER 1

Why Buy and Why Now

So you want to buy a house. And immediately, the questions start: What's my first step? Is it time to buy? How different is it today from five years ago? Is it better now, is it safe? Should I wait or just continue renting? How do I know if I am getting a good deal? What is a house really worth? How can I protect myself in this market? And then there is my favorite: How do I get me one of those foreclosures for a steal?

I get calls and e-mails asking these questions every single day, at work, at the coffee shop, backstage at TV talk shows when I am a guest, and when I lecture around the country at real estate and wealth expos.

Buying a house is the largest financial investment most people will make in their lifetimes, yet the vast majority of homebuyers are completely unprepared for the process. And to make matters worse, what has completely befuddled potential homebuyers in today's market has been the recent insanity surrounding real estate. The skyrocketing appreciation of home prices followed by the plummeting of values and the collapse of the subprime market has led to the flood of foreclosures and short sales.

Even in the best and most stable of market conditions, one mistake or misstep can result in a missed opportunity and thousands of dollars in unnecessary higher costs, fees, expenses, and bottom-line prices. I see homebuyers overpay, overspend, and get trapped into houses they can't afford all the time. They are either paralyzed by or fall prey to an unfamiliar and somewhat terrifying process. It doesn't have to be that way.

The Good News

The good news is that today's market offers unprecedented opportunities for homebuyers—if you understand today's market and the new rules. After the explosion of bad decisions, overspending, and badly structured mortgage programs, the smoke has cleared to reveal a new market of real estate standards and practices that provides a safer, more secure, and healthier climate for homebuyers and homeowners.

You Need a Road Map Before You Buy in This New Market

As the market continues to change around us, pitfalls and land mines still remain. This book provides homebuyers in today's market a precise road map to avoid them and arrive successfully at homeownership. The coming chapters present the keys to unlocking the secrets to buying safe, buying sane, and buying smart.

In today's economy you need to make your purchasing dollars go further—allowing you to buy more house for less money—all the while finding and selecting the house you can actually afford. But most important, you have to know how to avoid the mistakes of homebuyers of the past decade. You must learn the honest, hype-free pros and cons of homeownership, secure a mortgage that is safe and stable, and purchase a home that fits both your lifestyle and your budget.

A Step-by-Step Process

From the time you decide to buy a house to the day you move into your new home, you'll watch the months fly by. There is so much to do, so many things to think about. It's exciting and overwhelming all at once.

But don't worry. Even in today's market, buying a home is a pretty linear process. It is rather orderly and very much a step-by-step procedure. By knowing what to expect and what to do during each phase, you will walk through it with ease and success. So keep this book on your nightstand from day one. It will guide you each step of the way.

Home Buying—Step by Step

- Decide to buy

- Get your finances in order

- Get preapproved for a mortgage

- Decide what kind of house to buy and where to live

- Select your real estate agent

- Complete the three-step house shopping process

- Make your initial offer

- Negotiate

- Get your final offer accepted

- Open escrow

- Coordinate the three closing arenas

- Secure your mortgage

- Sign the closing paperwork

- Pick up the keys and move in

Why Buy a Home?

Why buy a home? The best way I can answer that is to share a story.

I was having dinner with a very good friend of mine, Rich. He's a successful screenwriter, having written sequels to many of Disney's most popular movies. Rich was interested in buying his first condo. He had been renting for the past ten years in Santa Monica, California, but recently started mulling over the idea of buying. While he is a genius at creating stories about princesses and flying carpets, he really doesn't know anything about real estate. He was concerned because he'd recently read an article stating plainly that buying a home was not a smart or good place to put your money.

I flatly disagreed, then took a bite of my salad. I offered him an explanation. I asked him how much rent he was paying per month. Twenty-five hundred dollars, he replied. I then asked him about the price tag on the condo he had just viewed the day before. It was priced at $300,000. I quickly calculated that with a 20 percent down payment, his total monthly costs, including mortgage, maintenance, taxes, and insurance, would be approximately $2,500. Wow, how surprising: it was just about the same as he was currently paying in rent.

Our food was getting cold, but I really wanted to bring my point home, so to speak. So I took my calculations further and told him that if he purchased the condo the following day, for the next thirty years he'd be paying $2,500 a month, at which point it would be paid off and he'd own it free and clear. Even if the market didn't appreciate one bit over the next thirty years—which would be virtually impossible given the history of long-term real estate trends—he would have $300,000 in equity. And he could then sell it and pocket the cash.

By comparison, if he were to continue dishing out $2,500 per month in rent, at the end of those thirty years he would have zero dollars in equity—nothing, zip! Rich's landlord would be rich, but Rich wouldn't be.

Rich stared at me for a moment, took in this information, nodded his head, and said, "Okay, I get it." I finished my salad and he started in on his pork chop.

Owning a Home Is a Win on Many Levels

The long-term financial benefits of buying a home are unparalleled, and the advantages go beyond just those related to money. Home ownership is a win on two levels—financial and lifestyle.

1. Seven financial benefits
2. Seven lifestyle benefits

The Seven Financial Benefits

Indeed, there's no place like home. We are going to talk about all the reasons that homeownership is part of the fabric of our lifestyle in a moment, but let's first see how it makes sense. Or should I say, makes "cents"—money and financial stability. Let's start by examining the classic reasons why buying a home is clearly the first step on the road to financial security and independence, no matter what the market is doing.

1. Homeownership Builds Wealth Over Time

We were always taught growing up that owning a home is financially savvy. Our parents knew it. But this past decade of real estate turbulence has shaken everyone's confidence. That is why it's so important that we discuss this; it is the first "New Rule for Today's New Market." A rule that just happens to be new and old at the same time.

New Rule: Homeownership Builds Wealth Over Time

Well, here's a big shocker: over the past forty years home values have actually appreciated at an average of approximately 4 percent a year! I know, I know, it's hard to believe, but it's true. While short-term market conditions can fluctuate dramatically, housing continues to represent a strong long-term investment.

Since the 1960s, national median existing-home prices have averaged a 4 percent overall rise per year. And that range of time includes all the skyrocketing values and equally turbulent recessions and periods of sales decline.

In short, even taking into account the significant drop in home prices in most markets over the past five years, a buyer who purchased a home before 2003 would very likely still sell for a profit today. Thus even considering the recent monumental highs and lows of the market, the 4 percent increase over forty years has stayed true to form.

Median and Average Sales Prices of New Homes Sold in United States
1963-2010 Annual Data

If you go back to 1963, you'll find that average home prices were $25,000. In the second quarter of 2010, the median single-family home price was approximately $178,800, according to the National Association of Realtors. That's an increase in value of approximately 700 percent, or an average of around 4.5 percent a year—up and down markets included.

Take a look at the graph above. If you were to look closer at the ride between 1963 and 2010, you'd notice some peaks and valleys along the way. Then a big rise and fall between 2003 and 2010. But you can clearly see that until approximately 2003 there was a slow and steady increase in the average price of a home. Short-term real estate prices may go up and down, but average overall real estate prices increase over time. In the long term you can see there is a continual upward trend. Peaks and valleys are correction periods, such as what began in 2006. The good news is that these corrections help the real estate market reestablish itself and gather momentum once again, ultimately moving it upward.

The numbers for the chart on the next page come from the Office of Federal Housing Finance Agency's Web site. It calculates the home values and total rates of appreciation for the cities listed. The chart reflects the increase in value of a home purchased for $250,000 in 1990 and held through 2010.

Home Price Appreciation from 1990 to 2010 for Select Cities				
City	State	Initial Value	Ending Value	Total Appreciation (%)
Atlantic City	NJ	$250,000	$555,000	121%
Anchorage	AK	$250,000	$583,000	133%
Billings	MT	$250,000	$664,000	166%
Boston	MA	$250,000	$575,000	130%
Boulder	CO	$250,000	$739,000	196%
Charleston	SC	$250,000	$617,000	147%
Chicago	IL	$250,000	$477,000	91%
Cheyenne	WY	$250,000	$615,000	146%
Denver	CO	$250,000	$704,000	182%
Des Moines	IA	$250,000	$488,000	95%
Honolulu	HI	$250,000	$451,000	80%
Huntsville	AL	$250,000	$444,000	78%
Kansas City	MO	$250,000	$477,000	91%
Las Vegas	NV	$250,000	$332,000	33%
Medford	OR	$250,000	$635,000	154%
Midland	TX	$250,000	$591,000	136%
Miami	FL	$250,000	$589,000	136%
New York	NY	$250,000	$627,000	151%
Raleigh	NC	$250,000	$486,000	94%
Salt Lake City	UT	$250,000	$716,000	186%
San Antonio	TX	$250,000	$510,000	104%

Source: Office of Federal Housing Finance Agency

What this all means is that if you bought a home in Salt Lake City in 1990 for $250,000, in 2010 it was worth $716,000. Even with all the ups and downs of the past ten years, that $250,000 house was worth $716,000—a 186 percent increase in value over those twenty years. Amazing long-term wealth building. Even in the cities that had been hit the hardest with decreases in property values and economic slowdown these past five years, such as Las Vegas or Huntsville, Alabama, there is a price appreciation of 33 percent to 78 percent over this twenty-year period.

2. You Build Equity Every Month

Your equity in your home is the amount of money you can sell it for minus what you still owe on it. Every month you make a mortgage payment, and every month a portion of what you pay reduces the amount you owe. That reduction of your mortgage every month increases your equity. The way mortgages work, the principal portion of your payment increases slightly every month year after year. It's lowest on your first payment and highest on your last payment. Thus, as the months and years go by, your equity grows.

3. You Reap Tax Benefits

- **Mortgage deduction:** The tax code allows homeowners to deduct the mortgage interest from their tax obligations. For many people this is a huge deduction since interest payments can be the largest component of your mortgage payment in the early years of owning a home.

- **Some closing cost deductions:** The first year you buy your home, you are able to claim the points (also called origination fees) on your loan, no matter whether they are paid by you or the seller. And because origination fees of 1 percent or more are common, the savings are considerable. Chapter 14 will review all these for you in detail.

- **Property tax is deductible:** Real estate property taxes paid on your primary residence and a vacation home are fully deductible for income tax purposes.

- **Interest on home equity loans:** In addition to your mortgage interest you can deduct the interest you pay on a home equity loan (or line of credit). This allows you to shift your credit card debts to your home equity loan, pay a lower interest rate than the horrendously exorbitant credit card interest rates, and get a deduction on the interest as well.

4. You Get a Capital Gains Exclusion

If you buy a home to live in as your primary residence for more than two years then you will qualify. When you sell, you can keep up to $250,000 if you are single, or $500,000 if you are married, in profit, and not owe any capital gains taxes. Now, it may sound ridiculous that your house could be worth more than when you purchased it after these past several years of falling house prices. However, as we have discussed, if you purchased your home anytime prior to 2003, chances are it has appreciated in value and this tax benefit will come in very handy. Oh, by the way, we will see appreciation of home prices in the years to come as well.

5. You Can Use Home Equity as Leverage

Building up equity in your home allows you eventually to leverage that equity to pay for other expenses in life. And as we just discussed, unlike interest payments made on a credit card balance, home equity loan interest payments are deductible. For many homeowners, it makes sense to pay off this kind of debt with a home equity loan. Though some states restrict use of home equity loans, you can typically borrow against your home's equity for a variety of reasons, including to make home improvements, pay for an education, cover medical bills, or start a small business. But be warned:

> **New Rule: A Home Equity Loan or Line of Credit Is Not a Bottomless Piggy Bank**
>
> Just because you have available equity in your house, be very conservative when you pay off your credit card bills or borrow against an equity line of credit. Too many homeowners treated their homes like piggy banks to crack open anytime they wanted to take a vacation, buy a new car, or pay for college tuition. When home prices dropped they found themselves equity poor and in trouble.

6. A Mortgage Is Like a Forced Savings Plan

Paying that mortgage every month and reducing the amount of your principal is like a forced savings plan. Each month you are building up more valuable equity in your home. In a sense, you are being forced to save—and that's a good thing.

7. Long Term, Buying Is Cheaper than Renting

In the first years it may be cheaper to rent. As we just discussed, in the first few years, most of your monthly mortgage payment goes toward interest. But over time as the interest portion of your mortgage payment decreases, the interest that you pay will eventually be lower than the rent you would have been paying. But more important, you are not throwing away all that money on rent. You gotta live someplace, so instead of paying off your landlord's home or building, pay off your own!

Bonus Benefit: Inflation Protection

Homeownership offers some inflation protection. No, it's not perfect. But studies by renowned economics professor Karl "Chip" Case and others suggest that, over the long term, housing has tended to beat inflation by a couple of percentage points a year. That's valuable inflation insurance, especially if you're young and raising a family and thinking about the next thirty or forty years. This hedge against inflation gives homeownership a bonus benefit.

The Seven Lifestyle Benefits

The importance of real estate goes well beyond the value of a dollar. For many people, owning a home marks a significant step on the path to achieving the American Dream. However, financial gain is not the only factor to consider when thinking about buying a home. You are investing in yourself, your family, your future, and your lifestyle.

A home is the place where life happens. It's the primary setting for making and sharing memories; raising families; celebrating happy occasions; or regrouping in the face of life's inevitable challenges. We *live* in our homes—not just in today's market value or tomorrow's interest rate. Let's look at the seven lifestyle benefits that are the most significant.

> Homeownership is in our DNA. People don't say, "When I grow up I want to get married, start a family . . . and *rent*."
> —Jim Gillespie

1. Pride of Ownership

Pride of ownership is possibly the greatest lifestyle benefit of all when it comes to owning a home. The feelings of accomplishment, safety, and security that result from homeownership cannot be matched by any other purchase or investment. According to the National Association of Realtors, even in a downward-moving market, lifestyle choice and pride of ownership are still strong incentives for homeownership, and consumers continue to move and purchase homes for lifestyle, despite the economy.

2. Shelter

You know the old truism: ya gotta live someplace. Shelter is a basic need of human beings, yet the benefit is often overlooked in the home-buying process. Remember, a home is a place where one lives and raises a family. Thus, it's the only investment you can actually live in!

3. Independence

A key difference between renting and owning is the flexibility a homeowner has in adapting a living space to individual tastes and needs. That means being able to decorate, renovate, landscape, and add personal touches to one's surroundings—without having to check in with a landlord first. Home improvements also increase the value of a home, making "independence" a personal *and* financial benefit of homeownership.

4. Stability

You are your own landlord, which gives you a feeling of control and financial stability. Once you secure a stable, fixed-rate mortgage you'll know exactly what your payments will be each month throughout the term of your mortgage. This enables you to budget and plan for other things you'll want to do in life. While certain factors such as property taxes may slightly fluctuate in some communities, the bulk of home-related expenses will remain stable and predictable as well.

5. Feeling of Community

When you buy a home, you buy a share in a community—a social benefit rarely experienced by renters, who are often considered transient, even after living in the same place for many years. Developing friendships with neighbors and feeling one has a place in the community fosters a safe and secure environment for oneself and one's family.

6. Improved Quality of Life

The benefits of homeownership go well beyond the obvious financial and the clear lifestyle benefits listed above. It's been statistically proven that these lifestyle benefits extend beyond you, to your partner or spouse, your children, and your community. According to the U.S. Department of Housing and Urban Development (HUD), homeowners will:

- Accumulate more wealth than do renters as the investment in their homes grows
- Enjoy better living conditions
- Have children who tend, on average, to do better in school
- Have family members who are less likely to become involved with crime
- Experience better overall physical health of individual household members

7. Safer Neighborhoods

What's more, communities benefit from the stable neighborhoods homeowners create. The NAR recently published a paper, "Social

Benefits of Homeownership and Stable Housing," showing that homeownership lowers neighborhood crime rates and homeowners are more involved in their communities—participating more in civic affairs.

Know What Went Wrong to Know What's Right Now

So with all that is great about homeownership, how could things have gone so terribly wrong over the past ten years? Well, there were a lot of contributing factors all coming together to create the perfect storm: a seemingly unending availability of home loans to unqualified buyers, crazy overdevelopment, overpaying, insane house pricing, 20 percent yearly home-price increases, wide-scale underfinancing, and subprime lending with ballooning interest-only payments. Risking everything, leveraging all you own, and buying houses with none of your own money were all common practices. It's a dangerous indicator when houses become so overpriced that no one can afford them. Add in all the subprime loans that should never have been issued to people who really couldn't afford the top-of-the-market prices. Then throw into the mix the developers who overbuilt. They sold new homes and con-dos to speculators who bought preconstruction properties in hopes of selling them for a premium upon completion. When all these factors collided, the market was bound to collapse. And it did.

In order to understand where things stand today, it is important to know what went wrong. These nine issues seem to have been the main players.

The Nine Nasty Sins of the Market Crash

1. Everyone Wanted a Piece of the American Dream

Demand for home purchases hit new peaks in the early 2000s—especially in light of an overall healthy economy, low interest rates, and lenders who began to make mortgage money available to those who may not have qualified in the past. As big real estate profits became big news, more Americans jumped into the home-buying market and it became a vicious cycle. As even more buyers raced in, home prices skyrocketed artificially, which then created a frenzy among buyers and speculators desperate to cash in on the ever-appreciating market. Thus the vicious cycle rolled on.

2. People Believed That Prices Would Keep Rising Forever

Hand in hand with this growth in buyer demand came the misconception that home prices—and home equity—would continue to rise indefinitely, which in turn brought more buyers-as-speculators into the market. Ultimately, this "too good to be true" scenario turned out to be just that.

3. Homes Became Lottery Tickets—Cash Jackpots

Homeowners and banks became obsessed in the newly inflated investment value of homes. A house became much more than a home—it became a winning lottery ticket. Owners borrowed against their newfound equity to fund renovations, travel, college educations, and expensive cars. Banks refinanced and wrote out big checks for huge equity lines. People spent all this newly acquired cash. And when home prices plummeted, they were left owing more than their houses were worth.

4. Creation of High-Risk Loans

To meet the demand of many new buyers, lenders created and made available a broad range of nontraditional mortgage options, including adjustable rate mortgages (ARMs), interest-only loans, and loans with initial teaser rates. Appropriately nicknamed "liar loans," these teaser-rate mortgages had artificially low initial rates that later grew, ballooning the payment to two or three times its starting size within two to five years.

"Payment-option" ARMs allowed buyers to choose how much they paid each month. Some of these allowed the buyer to pay the interest only, or in some cases, less than the interest, allowing for artificially low early-stage payments. This enabled buyers to qualify for bigger loans that in time they ultimately could not afford.

5. Subprime Lenders and Greedy Banks

In addition to the new mortgage products, banks and other lenders began to expand their lending practices to include buyers with little or poor or no credit histories. These unqualified buyers, often with undocumented incomes, composed the so-called subprime buyer market. Had the banks wanted to scrutinize these buyers under traditional rules and standards for a loan, they would never have qualified.

Just like the ARM loans, these subprime loans frequently had lower payments to start, but then adjusted higher. However, these programs carried even higher interest rates to make up for the perceived risk posed by these less than eligible borrowers. As these already high rates adjusted even higher, coupled with a decline in home prices, the underqualified borrower became unable to make payments and could not sell the home quickly enough to recover financially.

So when the market took a tumble, so did these unprepared and underfinanced buyers. Eventually they defaulted on their mortgages, adding to a tidal wave of "bad" mortgages that crippled the entire financial system and brought down a proverbial house of cards.

6. Buyers Rushed In and Didn't Do Their Homework

The banks and the lenders are not the only ones at fault here. Homebuyers have to take some responsibility here, too. I can't tell you how many homebuyers I questioned who had no idea what interest rate they were paying, what kind of loan they had, and if their low payment was due to adjust anytime soon. I was always taught never to sign anything that I didn't fully understand. In some cases, questionable lending practices and a lack of transparency were at fault. But bottom line: buyers didn't read the fine print and were unwilling to believe that if it seems too good to be true . . . it is!

7. Unbridled Speculation

Speculators jumped into the market and snapped up as many newly constructed condos and preconstruction homes as possible. Delighted developers stepped up production to meet demand. Speculators would put very little money down to lock in new construction units, and then resell them for huge profits even before they were finished. In boom markets like South Florida, Las Vegas, and San Diego, market appreciation of 40 to 50 percent set the stage for big returns. But when the market started to fall apart, speculators and the developers were left holding the bag and began defaulting on properties by the thousands—contributing to the market fallout even further.

8. Rewards for Bad Behavior

In the height of the real estate boom, more people began to secure mortgages from independent brokers—some of whom received bonuses or incentives for steering buyers toward higher-risk loan products. Unfortunately, it's been documented that in some cases, lenders downplayed the benefits of traditional loans in favor of the higher-risk products.

9. Lack of Government Regulation

And last, not that it is ultimately the government's job to police the lending institutions and the financial sector, but did it turn a blind eye? Clearly the lending institutions were not going to regulate themselves and adhere to the time-tested lending requirements and qualifying requirements. In spite of the fact that more borrowers entered the market, and more were taking advantage of higher-risk options, the Federal Reserve did very little to exercise oversight on the market. Even though the Fed recommends that lenders must scrutinize borrowers' ability to make long-term payments and it advocates improving education to consumers, these suggestions clearly fell on deaf ears.

Understanding Today's New Market

Now that the dust has settled from this last decade of real estate deca-dence, what *is* this new market that has arisen out of the ashes?

First let me say that I, as well as many other experts, believe that any bubble burst and huge market downturn in an overinflated and out-of-control market is a good thing.

For several years I made numerous guest appearances on *Larry King Live*. One night on the show alongside Donald Trump, Barbara Corcoran, and Robert Kiyosaki, Larry asked us all, "Is a sinking real estate market a horrendous precursor for the future of real estate?" Every one of us explained that a major downtown in the market was a very good thing. It is a natural correction of what was an otherwise runaway, escalating, unending, overinflated market. There was a re-sounding agreement from all of us. But why would all four of Larry's "esteemed" experts agree on this topic?

We, along with many real estate experts, recognize that the big market correction of 2007 to 2010, and the massive downturn in home prices, has made buying a home safer, more secure, and, most important . . . more affordable.

I know it's hard for many ho-meowners and investors whose properties are or were "upside down" to see a positive outcome from a downward market swing. But these downturns are necessary corrections. They help bring the highly inflated levels of pricing and speculation back in line with the salary range of the average buyer and investor. These inflated markets needed the correction. They needed "Today's New Market."

> We are experiencing a return to the more traditional lending standards that were in effect before the housing boom—lending standards that support a stable economic environment for both homebuyers and the nation at large.
>
> —Jim Gillespie

The New Rules for Today's New Market

Buying a home that you simply can't afford is now taboo in this now smarter, more conservative, and ultimately healthier market. It's one that takes the pendulum swing back toward prudence and restraint. How buyers buy, guidelines for bigger down payments, and qualifications for mortgages have all become more stringent.

The year 2000 marked the beginning of the wild era of over-speculation. It was a decade of real estate investing on crack! The traditional rules of home buying were ignored, disregarded, and abandoned. All the classic rules that had been the guidelines for the past forty years were cast aside, and a whole new way of real estate investing emerged. What was the outcome of this complete disregard for the classic time-tested rules of home buying? The outcome is the "New Rules for Today's New Market."

I know that I am dating myself when I say this, but many of these new rules are old rules . . . tried-and-true rules that have been around for decades. Many of the new rules I will discuss throughout this book are based on the classic and conservative, solid home-buying rules that I've followed since I began buying properties back in 1979. These New Rules for Today's New Market are critical for every homebuyer, homeowner, and real estate investor. Learn them and play by them, and you will have a safe, secure, and satisfying home-buying experience.

It's Only on Paper Till You Sell

Back in 2006, people became overnight millionaires because of their home's sudden increase in value. I was warning people then not to get too crazy and start spending like a millionaire because their wealth was only really on paper! And unless they were planning to cash out, drop out, and move to Belize, they were going to have to buy something else at an equally inflated price!

Just as you can become an overnight millionaire on paper, the exact opposite is true when the market goes down and your house loses all that overinflated value it had artificially gained. It is still only on paper. You gained it on paper and you lost it on paper.

Think of your home and its value the same way you think of stocks. Your house is only worth what you can sell it for today. When the stock market tanks, is that the time to sell? When so many of us got our stock statement back in 2008 and our portfolio had dropped by 50 percent, did we run out and sell everything off? No, we hoped that eventually the market would slowly, painfully climb its way back up. It happened to me; I saw my stock portfolio value cut in half. But the professionals reassured me that it didn't matter unless I was planning to sell.

The same holds true with a home. Even if the market turns south, if you don't have to sell it immediately and are in it for the long term, you are secure.

My "Only on Paper" Success—Yours, Too

I am going to give you a great example of how buying a home to live in is a long-term winner and why you should just relax and trust that markets go up and down. I bought a gorgeous home in Palm Springs, California, back in 2002. At the time it seemed like a good deal. It was priced at $749,000. It was 4,000 square feet located on what was to become a beautiful golf course.

With the help of my good negotiating skills and the techniques I will explain in this book, I was able to shave $50,000 off the asking price of $749,000 and pay $699,000. The years passed, and the market went crazy. At one point the house was estimated to be worth $1,250,000. The house was a gold mine! . . . on paper. More years went by, and the market tanked. The identical house next door sold for $850,000. Well, to the novice homeowner or investor, I just lost a bundle. My house went from $1.2 million to $850,000. How tragic. But it's not. That inflated value of the house was never my money. It was not a real value, it was just that—inflated. My house is now worth $850,000, which is $150,000 more than what I paid for it eight years ago. Even taking into account the manic highs and lows of the market in this last decade, my home still appreciated in value over the long term. So will yours.

Why Buy Now

Okay, it looks like we have now come full circle to answer the big question that began this chapter: why buy and why now?

The great news is that today's market is a fantastic time to buy a house. This is the smartest time to buy a home in the thirty-five years that I have been involved in real estate. Excellent prices, low interest rates, government and tax incentives, and lots of choices.

The Top Five Reasons to Buy Now

The first four reasons to buy are summed up in a very easy and simple formula.

Jim Gillespie of Coldwell Banker likes to call it the "Triple I—P" effect. When all these factors combine they create an amazing buying opportunity.

The Triple I—P

I = Inventory

I = Interest Rates

I = Incentives

P = Price

---

1. **Huge *inventory* of home and properties**—In most markets around the nation, home inventory has increased, giving buyers a greater choice. Foreclosures and short sales abound. We've already hit the bottom in the vast majority of markets, so there's never been a better time to swoop in and get a great deal.

2. ***Interest rates***—At the same time, mortgage rates remain at near historic lows and home prices have decreased over the last three years, which is the first time that has happened since World War II.

3. **Government and tax and seller** *incentives*—Not only are the prices great, but the terms are better right now, with many deals offering additional credits toward closing costs. Incentives like federal tax credits have been hitting the books, and individual realty companies have been offering their own incentive packages. And don't forget the built-in tax advantages of homeownership that we just discussed . . . the ultimate incentive.

4. **Great** *prices*—Prices dropped about 2 percent in 2007, 9.3 percent in 2008, 12.4 percent in 2009, and approximately 2 percent in 2010 in many areas, according to the National Association of Realtors. In some areas of the country we have seen prices drop up to 30 percent over the past few years. The bottom line? No matter where in the country you are, houses are just plain less expensive.

There's one more reason to buy a home today that adds to the Triple I—P:

5. *Motivated sellers*—A lot of sellers are sitting on properties they want to get rid of. If they are individual homeowners, they most likely purchased a home they ultimately can't afford. Or they secured an initial mortgage with risky terms that has now become unmanageable. Or they have experienced a job loss due to the economy and can't come up with the monthly payment. If the property is now owned by the bank, you can bet it is a motivated seller, with a long list of properties it needs to unload.

"The Perfect Storm" of Buying Opportunity

Probably the best reason to buy now is that all parties concerned are learning from their mistakes. Guidelines and more stringent qualifiers are now in place. And homebuyers have learned to buy only what they can afford. Home buying in this new market is a better, more conservative, safer, and more reliable way to build financial stability for you and your family. And I, for one, am very happy about that!

So you have the Triple I—P, and you have lots of motivated sellers. You also now have new consumer-protecting safeguards in place. All of this creates an almost perfect storm of buying opportunity. It allows for something that the real estate market has not seen in a decade: home affordability. Now, there's a term most of us have not heard in years.

So there you have it, the answer to the question proposed by this first chapter: why buy, why now?

Let's go buy a house!

What You Learned in This Chapter

♦ Buying a home has unparalleled benefits for you both financially and lifestyle-wise.

♦ The market naturally goes through ups and downs, and despite the short-term highs and lows, there is long-term house price appreciation.

♦ Buying a home for the long term is safe, secure, and sensible.

♦ You can protect yourself from the pitfalls that other homeowners experienced in the last decade by following the New Rules for Today's New Market.

PART TWO

Preparing to Buy

CHAPTER 2

How Much

I like the title of this chapter because it initiates so many important questions. How much is it going to cost? How much money do I need? How much house can I afford? How much down payment should I have? And ... how much more will it cost me to buy than to continuing renting?

Rent vs. Buy

I want to teach you step by step how to buy a house in today's market. But if you are currently renting, are you really *ready* to buy? The one big decision you have to make if you are renting now is: should you change things up and become a homeowner?

By this point in the book, you know the solid financial and life-style benefits to home buying. But perhaps a part of you still subscribes to the idea that it's better and easier to rent rather than make the jump to homeownership. Well, perhaps you need an objective nudge to push you over to the homeowner's side.

Why Make Your Landlord Rich?

The reality is that when you rent you pay someone else's mortgage. You pay your landlord's mortgage. He's getting rich because you are paying off the mortgage on his house or building.

I am a landlord, so I know. I own some rental property. One building in particular has very nice high rents. From $2,000 to $2,400 per month for large one-bedroom units. Yes, it's a very, very nice building with beautiful apartments. One of my tenants has lived there for well over ten years. Do you realize how much money she has paid me, that I in turn have used to pay off my mortgage? Let's do the math: $2,000 per month x 12 months x 10 years = $240,000. That seems insane to me. That's a lot of money! If that tenant had purchased a condo ten years ago, she would have a big chunk of it paid off by now.

On a positive note for renting, when you rent, you essentially deed the upkeep of the property and other responsibilities to the landlord. However, that's not always the case. I have many friends who rent apartments and are constantly fixing, repairing, and renovating their units because the landlords are more than happy to accept their monthly rents, but refuse to make any improvements.

I am always amused when friends brag to me about the improvements they have made to their apartments. They show me how beautiful their rental is, while bragging about the $5,000 they spent fixing up the unit, refinishing the floors, redoing the kitchen, etc. What a waste of their money. They are investing in someone else's building or home. Not their own!

Good Reasons *Not* to Buy

You know all the pros and the benefits. But now I am going to tell you adamantly that if you are not ready to buy, then don't! Never jump into the purchase of a home if you are not able to afford to buy at that moment. Yes, today's market makes this a fantastic time to buy. Great prices, great interest rates. But if you can't afford it . . . keep renting.

Four Reasons *Not* to Buy

1. **Not enough for the down payment**—You don't have significant savings yet for a healthy down payment. Down payments in today's market are far bigger and more significant than they have been in the past decade. I will talk a lot about how much you will *really* need later on in this chapter.

2. **Planning a move in the next three years**—Is a job transfer on the horizon? Are you getting hitched? Are you in a relationship that may result in marriage down the road? Or you are about to have a baby and will need a bigger place within a few years? If you would have to sell again relatively soon you could lose money. Generally, a home is not a good short-term investment because the transaction costs are too high. Yes, you will have been paying down some of your mortgage monthly, but when you factor in paying a Realtor between 4 and 6 percent of the sales price, this can amount to more than the average long-term annual national home price appreciation rate plus the equity you have accrued. So if you own a home for only a short time, you might end up paying more to sell it than you have gained.

3. **Short on income**—You don't have the income and salary to cover a house payment and carrying costs. Too often, first-time homebuyers equate their rent with the mortgage, mistakenly thinking they can buy a house if their mortgage payment is the same amount as rent. Actually, there are several more costs associated with a house, and these monthly expenses can be sizable: property taxes, insurance, maintenance, homeowner's dues, etc. Try putting yourself to the test and play house first. Every month, bank the amount that you'd have to pay if you owned a home. It's good practice so you'll be ready for the real thing. This is a great way to test your ability to come up with the ongoing monthly costs. After even two months of this you'll be able to tell if you are really ready for the jump.

4. **Questionable job security**—Is the handwriting on the wall? Is your company downsizing or laying people off in the near future? Your job's future is not certain. If things look bleak and prospects do not seem promising for your current job to con-

tinue, you should not make that big homeownership commitment just yet. Also bear in mind that most lenders will want
to see consistency in your professional history. This is not the
time to switch industries or decide to start your own company.
You'll likely have to show that you've been in the same job—in
the same industry—for at least a couple of years.

In summary, if any of the reasons not to buy apply to you, then
don't buy now! Just keep saving your cash. Because the more you save,
the bigger the down payment you will be able to make, and thus the
lower your monthly mortgage payment will be. That means you will
need less income to qualify for that loan. So just keep stashing that
cash!

Two Poor Excuses Not to Buy

You now know the legitimate reasons not to buy—but there are two
excuses I want to blow out of the water. Renters frequently cite these
as their top reasons not to buy. However, neither is a valid reason to
stay put and keep shelling out that cash each month for rent.

1. **Fear of the market**—You are paralyzed by the fear that the
   market won't appreciate in the long term and that in thirty
   years your house will be worth less than what you paid for it
   today. I think we have shown that this is a fear just simply not
   based in fact.

2. **Supercheap rent**—You have a really inexpensive rent-
   controlled apartment. However, if you continue to pay your
   rent-controlled apartment at $1,300 a month for, say, thirty
   years, you'll end up giving $468,000 to your landlord. And by
   the way, it's unrealistic to think your rent won't ever go up. So,
   what you have at the end of the day is more rental payments
   rather than a home that could be well on its way to being
   paid off.

BYB Tip: Uncle Sam May Give Some Back!

Keep in mind that even if you determine that the money you will spend on a mortgage and monthly maintenance is more than what you are currently spending on rent, when you factor in the mortgage interest deductions and real estate tax deductions, you may actually come out ahead each year. Get an accountant on the phone and find out.

How Much Money Will You Need?

I was giving an interview to a writer from the *Los Angeles Times*, and she asked me what is the biggest change that has taken place in this new market. My immediate response was, "Buyers now have to have the money to come up with a down payment!" Wow, what a concept. Funny, but in the 1970s and '80s that's just how it was. You had to come up with a respectable down payment to buy a house. It was not until 2000–2006 that the concept of no money down morphed from a high-risk investing strategy to a commonly accepted buyer practice.

New Rule: You Need Money to Buy a House!

—Matt Woolsey, senior reporter, Forbes.com

You need to come up with the cash to put down a legitimate deposit. This rule is pretty straightforward. No-money-down purchases—no way! Very little down, because you can barely afford the house to begin with—no way!

No money down can immediately put you into a negative-equity position—especially in a downward-moving market. The days of 100 percent financing are long gone. Jim Gillespie often uses the expression "You need to have some skin in the game." Meaning you need to have some money invested in your home when you buy it.

Assuming you've already made the decision to buy a house, undoubtedly the money question is probably foremost on your mind. One of the lessons that we all should have learned from the past decade is that in today's new market everyone needs to know, long before they begin their house shopping, exactly how much they are really going to need to buy a home.

Most people only think about the down payment. If they have enough for that, then they are on the fast track to homeownership. Well, unfortunately that is only one of the components to the how-much-money-will-you-need formula. I'm not trying to scare you, I'm trying to prepare you. There are actually two significant amounts that you will have to shell out for right up front, and then two chunks of money that will be ongoing month after month after month after month.

How Much—the Four Components to Your Money Needs

- Up-front funds
    - —Down payment
    - —Purchase/closing costs
- Ongoing costs
    - —Monthly mortgage payments
    - —Monthly carrying costs

The Up-Front Funds

When people think about buying a home, the first thing they say is, "I've saved enough for a down payment on a house and I am ready to buy!" Well, as I just said, there more expenses than just the down payment. There are lots of expenses, or closing costs, as well. The down payment plus the closing costs are what I call the up-front funds. Why do you need to know about them? Because you need to be prepared for them. You don't want to be caught short at closing time and begin your new home-owning experience playing catch-up.

Your Down Payment—the Case for 20 Percent

What exactly is the down payment? It's the amount of money that you, the buyer, kick in out of your own pocket, right at the start, toward the purchase of the house. But exactly how much do you need to put down?

New Rule: Put 20 Percent Down!

Here's my feeling about this: always try to put 20 percent down. Period. Okay, so there are a few exceptions to the rule that I'll explain, but for the most part the 20 percent rule sticks. I've been recommending 20 percent forever—since long before the market had its recent huge downward swing. But as so many people fell prey to the idea of putting less than 20 percent down in recent times, we have to talk about this because it's a big deal and something I feel very strongly about.

Seven Reasons to Put 20 Percent Down

1. **Improved chance that you will get the mortgage**—The first and biggest reason to come up with 20 percent down is that in today's new market, many banks won't give you a mortgage unless you come up with at least that much. The loan programs that once existed for 10, 5, and 0 percent down are not just not available.

2. **Skin in the game**—Twenty percent has been the norm forever. It really serves to ensure that the homebuyer has "skin in the game" and is financially viable for the homeownership responsibility.

3. **Smaller monthly mortgage payment**—More money down means you borrow less, which means you will have a smaller mortgage, which means you will have a smaller, more affordable mortgage payment.

4. **Lower interest rate**—The interest charged on a loan with 20 percent down is often lower than the interest on a loan with less money down. Your lower interest rate will save you thousands if not tens of thousands of dollars over the life of the loan.

5. **No private mortgage insurance (PMI)**—Putting 20 percent down allows you to avoid private mortgage insurance. Also called lender's mortgage insurance, PMI is extra insurance that lenders require from most homebuyers who obtain loans in which the down payment is less than 20 percent of the sales price or appraised value. Many lenders will even add a percentage that is like an insurance policy onto the mortgage interest rate.

6. **Instant equity building**—A significant down payment builds instant equity in your home. A 20 percent down payment immediately puts equity into a property when you purchase it. That down payment safeguards you if the market turns downward temporarily.

7. **Great saving skills**—Saving for a full 20 percent down is a great way to establish practical and healthy saving practices. If you have saved up for 20 percent down, you have probably learned how to manage your money wisely. That skill is going to come in very handy because, as we will discuss in a moment, the money outflow doesn't stop once the seller hands over the keys to the front door!

But I Can Buy a Bigger House with That Money!

Let's say you have $80,000 saved toward a down payment. You're wondering, why buy a $400,000 house with 20 percent down when you can buy an $800,000 with 10 percent down? Wow: more house, better neighborhood! Hey, that sounds like a deal. But it's not. The entire real estate market and our economy in general were affected by the number of homebuyers who artificially exaggerated their purchasing power with this thinking—buying properties with 15, 10, 5, or even 0 percent down, thinking they were getting more house for their money. But what really happened was that homebuyers purchased homes that were higher priced *and* far more expensive than what they could ultimately afford.

Here's an example of how much money you'll need for a 20 percent down payment on a $417,000 home. Your down payment will have to be $83,400, and your monthly mortgage payment at 6 percent on a 30-year fixed loan will be $2,000 per month.

Running the numbers: 20 percent down

$417,000 × .20 = $83,400 down payment

Monthly mortgage payment @ 6 percent (30-year fixed) = $2,000

If You Don't Have Enough for 20 Percent Down

If you are not able to buy a property because you can't scrape together a 20 percent down payment, then you have two choices:

1. Shop for a less expensive property.

2. Don't buy now—keep saving.

But don't despair if you are coming up short of that 20 percent benchmark for your dream house. The next chapter will help you to identify the house you can afford with the money you have.

Exception to the 20 Percent Rule?

Yes, yes, yes. Twenty percent is the preferred amount of your down payment. And I would be very happy if everyone who wanted to buy a home put that much down. But I do need to share one other option.

Loans backed by the Federal Housing Administration (FHA) require only 3.5 percent down, which can be a viable option *if*—let me repeat: *if*—you qualify. Three and a half percent is a big jump from 20 percent down. But here's why. FHA qualifications are now so stringent that you will only get this loan with a scant 3.5 percent down requirement if you are truly qualified. What's more, there are limits on how much you can borrow. In general, you're limited to a relatively small mortgage, an amount that's linked to the home prices in your area. To find the limits in your region, visit HUD's Web site at www.hud.gov.

Fortunately, the government has now put many much-needed regulations on FHA loans, and the issuers will meticulously check your entire financial picture. To qualify you, they must inspect your credit rating and your bank statements, and verify your employment and your income, to assess your ability to pay your monthly mortgage payments. So, if you decide to go this route, be forewarned that you'll be scrutinized even more thoroughly than with a 20 percent down loan.

Another downside to this small down payment is that you will then have a much higher monthly mortgage payment. Which also means you will need to show more yearly income and salary to qualify for this loan.

 BYB Tip: 3.5 Percent Down = Don't Buy Yet

Okay, now I have told you that there is an option out there for a loan that requires less than 20 percent down. However, here is my expert advice: if you qualify for an FHA loan, yet you can only come up with 3.5 percent for a down payment—you can't afford this house. Don't buy now—keep saving. I still stand strong that you should put 20 percent down, for all the reasons I discussed before. Your home purchase becomes safer, smarter, and more secure.

Your Purchase/Closing Costs

The purchase, or closing, costs include all the expenses incurred to buy the house: appraisal fees, loan application fees, loan broker fees, termite inspection reports, and structural inspection fees. These tend to average around half a percent of the purchase price. But don't forget, it's possible that you may have to pay a point or more (a point is equivalent to 1 percent of the loan amount) in mortgage loan fees when you get your loan, so include that amount as well in these purchase closing costs. I'll be going into much greater detail about closing costs in chapter 15, which includes a chart to show you all the various costs involved in a typical closing. But on a $630,000 home purchase (with 20 percent down), your loan amount would be $504,000. Your closing costs would be approximately $8,190. That includes $3,150 in costs and $5,040 from 1 point in fees.

Running the numbers: Closing costs

$630,000 × .005 = $3,150 (0.5% in closing costs)

$504,000 × .01 = $5,040 (1 point in mortgage fees)

Total closing costs = $8,190

The Ongoing Costs

Let's put it all on the table, folks—just so there are no surprises! You need to know exactly what it will *all* cost . . . before and after your purchase. And you need to be prepared. I am not going to bury this section somewhere at the back of the book. You need to know this right from the get-go. As I said, I want you to be ready to own, not get caught shorthanded and overdrawn at the bank once you walk away from the closing table. Just because you are the proud new owner doesn't mean you haven't stopped spending yet!

Nine Ongoing Homeowner Expenses

1. **Monthly mortgage**—You'll be able to figure out in advance what your monthly payments will be, given the price of the house, how much you're putting down, and the interest rate you're paying. There are lots of online mortgage calculators out there.

2. **Property taxes**—These are usually paid twice a year, but the property tax laws vary state by state and even by county. In Hunterdon County, New Jersey, for example, residents pay about 1.89 percent of their home's value to property taxes. In Westchester County, New York, homeowners pay about 1.45

percent of their home's value in property taxes. California residents, on the other hand, enjoy lower property taxes, typically around 1 percent of their original purchase price.

3. **Homeowner's insurance**—This varies by state, and region. Depending on where you live and what kind of coverage you buy, insurance can run you anywhere between $500 and $1,500 a year. It helps to bundle your homeowner's insurance with other types of insurance, like auto and life, using the same company, as it will often offer you discounts for doing so.

4. **Hazard insurance**—This entails covering for earthquakes, floods, or hurricanes, depending on your area of the country.

5. **Condo, co-op, or homeowners association fees**—If you own a condo, co-op, or town house, you'll pay an annual or monthly fee to maintain the building and grounds. Single-family homes can also have assessments if they are located in a particular area or subdivision with common property. You may also have these expenses if you purchase into a gated community with security guards, a swimming pool, tennis courts, clubhouse, playground, and so on. Look for more info on this in chapter 6.

6. **Utilities**—You are probably paying them anyway as a renter, but chances are they may be a bit more now that you are running an entire home. Think about gas, electric, water, sewer, and trash removal.

7. **Routine maintenance**—Things break; things wear out. It happens. You'll want to keep some emergency money handy for a leaky roof, plugged kitchen sink, or dripping hot water heater. You'll probably average a couple hundred bucks a month in these "unexpected" costs.

8. **Pool and yard care**—Depending on how much there is to maintain, such as a pool or a garden, you'll need to have money to cover these routine expenses. And even if you decide to take care of these things yourself, you'll still need to hire professionals for heavy-duty tree trimming on occasion

or fixing a problem with your pool's heating system, for example, when it breaks down.

9. **And don't forget: moving expenses and new furnishings—**
It's not an ongoing expense, but an expense after you close nonetheless. Even if you already own a lot of your own furniture, you will likely still need items like a washer and dryer, which will require additional budget.

What You Learned in This Chapter

♦ If you can't afford to buy just yet . . . keep renting.

♦ If your income, job security, and ability to keep up with regular house payments—plus ongoing maintenance costs—are not predictable and stable, or you are planning to move in the next three years, then now may not be the right time to buy. There are some legitimate reasons to keep renting.

♦ Come up with a 20 percent down payment. This is one of the best ways to buy safe, sane, and smart in today's market. A huge mistake is to underestimate the actual cost of what's going to be coming out of your pocket.

♦ Before you buy, you need to know exactly how much money you will need to have available. There are four components to your home-buying money needs, including both the up-front and the ongoing costs. Be prepared.

CHAPTER 3

How Much House Can You Afford—
with the Money You've Got?

O kay, now you have a basic idea of the kind of up-front money you need and the ongoing costs of homeownership. Already you may be thinking, yikes, do I really need that much? Yes, you do.

Let's ask the next question. Assuming you've got a stash of money reserved for buying . . . with the money you've got, how much house can you afford to buy? To answer that—you had better figure out exactly how much money you've got first!

Your Financial Snapshot—Take a Picture

It's time to take a cold, hard look at your finances. You have to do a straightforward review to determine how much money you've got and what your overall financial picture looks like. In essence, you are taking a personal inventory of all your assets and liabilities. You need to know how much you have and how you can best use that amount of cash, no matter how much you have amassed, to maximize your buying power.

When you take your financial snapshot, you have to start by being honest. You must be brutally honest about both your income and your savings. You need to first take a realistic financial picture of yourself. You need to list all savings accounts, IRAs, 401(k)s, and other retirement accounts, money markets, stock funds, etc., that you have. Go online or call and ask for a recent balance sheet of your funds.

Make a list of all of your accounts with their current balances. I personally do not recommend you touch your retirement accounts, especially those that have penalties for withdrawals, but you still want to have them included in your inventory. Do you have any high balances on your credit cards? How much do you owe on them? Student loans? Any other big debts? Eventually when you apply for a loan, the lender will ask for all of this information anyway, so it's best to have it all compiled now and know what all the numbers indicate. Don't forget to include the money you have lent out to family and friends. It may be time to dig up that promissory note.

New Rule: If You Can't Afford It, Don't Buy It

—Suze Orman, bestselling author and financial expert extraordinaire

Don't buy beyond what you can afford. It's easy to fall into that all-you-can-eat attitude when it comes to your first home purchase. You "want it all" when it comes to size, amenities, location, etc. But remember that your eyes may be bigger than your wallet.

Even in this new market with tighter lending restrictions, just because a bank or lender is willing to lend you the money to buy a house, that does not mean you can afford it! You have to be realistic, do your homework first, and buy within your means. If the only way to get into real estate is to take a loan out of your 401(k) plan, then you shouldn't be getting into the market just yet.

Count Up Your Cash and Other Liquid Funds

You have done your financial forensics. You have sorted through your accounts, cataloged all your assets, made a list of all the money you owe, including that thousand dollars you borrowed from your college roommate that you promised to pay back someday. You even took that ten-pound coin jar to the market to have your nickels counted. Now you should have a good idea of exactly what cash you have on hand, and what liquid funds you've got as well in the form of money market accounts and so on.

What Will Your Money Buy You?

Let's look at an example with hard numbers. My good friend Erin wants to buy a house that costs $525,000. She has saved $55,000 and can probably get a gift or loan of $35,000 from her mom. That's $90,000.

If a house is selling for $525,000, putting 20 percent down, she is going to need the following:

Buying a $525,000 house with a 20 percent down payment	
$105,000	20 percent down payment
+ $2,625	Closing costs
+ $4,200	Possible costs of 1 point on her $420,000 mortgage
$111,825	Total up-front costs
$90,000 cash – $111,825 costs = $21,825 still short	

Well, her $90,000 clearly isn't enough. So let's look at our two options when you don't have enough money on hand to safely and conservatively buy a house.

1. Shop for a less expensive property.

2. Don't buy now—keep saving.

Let's try option number one, shop for a less expensive house. Let's try a lower price tag and see if we can make the numbers work.

The up-front costs for a $350,000 house has the following breakdown:

> **Buying a $350,000 house with a 20% down payment**
>
> | | |
> |---|---|
> | $70,000 | 20% down payment |
> | + $1,750 | Closing costs |
> | + $2,800 | Possible costs of 1 point on her $280,000 mortgage |
> | = $74,550 | Total up-front costs |
>
> **$90,000 cash – $74,550 = $15,450 now available**

With $74,550 in up-front costs, Erin has $15,450 remaining from her $90,000 nest egg. This is great! It is so much better to have a buffer left over than to be struggling to cover the bills. It looks like a house that costs $350,000 or less is the more realistic place for Erin to start. It may not be her ultimate dream house, but Erin shouldn't get discouraged—and neither should you. There are great deals out there, and you can always work your way up the property ladder as you build equity in this house over time. It's just that: a place to start.

Where Do I Get the Down Payment?

So you have run the numbers, and you think you realistically may have enough cash saved up. Fantastic! Good for you. But what if you find that you come up short? Then the next question you will ask me is, "Where can I get more money to put toward my down payment? I just don't think I have enough."

Coming up with enough money is a formidable first hurdle. You've gotten your finances in order so that you have a clear picture of what money you have. Now what?

There are lots of other factors that can enhance your down payment and your buying power as well. Here are several safe and sensible ways to make your buying power as big as possible.

Nine Ways to Build Your Down Payment and Boost Your Buying Power

1. Get a Little Help from Mom and Dad

A great and often overlooked source is . . . the folks. If your parents are in a position to help you, they can "gift" you money each year, tax free. The old maximum was $10,000 a year. Now it's $12,000 per year, *per parent*. That's $24,000 a year that can be gifted to you tax free from your parents. If you are married, you can double that to $48,000 a year. And if you are smart and plan ahead, two years' worth totals $96,000, a very nice start.

Taking personal loans from family is very acceptable. If you don't think your parents will help you out, approach them like a businessperson and ask for a loan that you'll pay back at a rate better than what they could get from a bank or in a money market account. The rate you'll pay would likely be less than the going rate from your own lending institution, which makes it win-win for everybody.

 BYB Buyer's Blunder: Borrowing More from Family Than You Can Handle

Be careful of the trap of borrowing more cash than you bargained for. If your parents are lucky enough to be in a position to lend you a sum for a healthy down payment, you don't want to get in over your head and buy an unnecessarily more expensive house with a bigger mortgage. Despite that nice down payment, you don't want your monthly mortgage payment to be too high. Be warned, some lenders in today's market may hesitate to lend to you if you come in with a big borrowed down payment and not enough income to support your monthly obligations.

And don't forget to factor that additional repayment amount to Mom and Dad into your ongoing monthly budget.

---

2. Pay Yourself First

Try setting aside money to be saved automatically every time you receive a paycheck—no matter what. Create a special savings account and have the money directly deposited. You will be shocked at how quickly your funds will grow. The secret to making a savings account grow is to make identical deposits at the same time every month. For example, if you are paid every two weeks and put aside $250 from every paycheck, at the end of twelve months, you will have saved $6,000.

3. Tighten Up—Put a Curb on Your Spending

Money expert David Bach, bestselling author of *Start Late, Finish Rich*, calls this the "latte factor." David and I were on tour together last year speaking to crowds all around the country. He talked about this practical and logical concept in his speeches. Cut back on your spending, chiefly on items that you really don't need, like designer coffee every morning or lunch and dinner out four or five days a week. If you can knock off 10 percent of your frivolous spending, that will add up to a nice sum saved.

4. Give a Friend a Hand

You've had friends come to you for money before, and for far less worthy endeavors than your first property. Maybe it's time for a little payback. Can one of your friends offer you a short-term loan at a fair interest rate? Someone just might surprise you.

5. Take a Part-Time or Second Job

It's amazing how a little extra income can add up over time. A friend of mine taught high school for years and owned an amazing home. When I asked him how he was able to purchase and afford an expensive home in a wonderful neighborhood, he said he had taken on a job part-time as a copywriter for a local paper, three nights a week. He allocated all of the money he earned as a writer to the purchase of his house. Over time, that little savings account grew and grew and grew. That extra $100 a night grew to over $15,000 in just one year.

By the way, he told me an extra bonus of the second job is that he was able to save more of his teaching salary, as he had less time to spend money on entertainment because he was working more!

Think also about seasonal or specialty work such as over the summer, during tax season, or from Thanksgiving to Christmas.

6. Save Your Tax Refund

If you're not a dedicated saver, try changing your withholding exemptions from one to zero. You'll see your paycheck shrink a little, but you'll get a bigger tax refund that you can then put toward your down payment.

7. If You Are a Renter, Get a Roommate

This one is a no-brainer—if you have an extra room, fill it. Let your apartment or your current home work for you. Get a roommate and sock away that extra income to bolster your seed money.

8. Possibly Tap a Retirement Account

In the new market, it's not a good idea to touch these funds. And, as most Americans have watched their investment accounts dwindle, this may not be an ideal source for you to tap anyway. But ask your accountant for details and options you may have with your retirement accounts. You may be able to withdraw money early from your IRA, 401(k), or other retirement account for the sole purpose of buying your first home. Rules, taxes, and penalties do apply. But if you are counting on these funds for your down payment, I would be cautious. Recalling Suze Orman's advice in the "New Rule" on page 41: if you have to borrow against your 401(k), then you can't afford to buy a house just yet.

9. Follow My Ten-Year Rule

This is my new prod for incentivizing saving. The principle behind it is very simple. Spending $25 on something twice a week may not seem like a big expenditure, even over the course of a month or two. Multiplying the cost over a full year may not even be shocking enough to jolt you out of an unnecessary spending habit. But do the math over ten years . . . and bam! You are looking at an astonishing amount of money.

A friend of mine has been hiring a personal trainer for more than two years now. He trains twice a week at $60 a session. I asked him if it was necessary . . . really. He said that, yes, he could work out on his own, but "it's only sixty dollars," so it's no big deal. Well, I slammed him with my ten-year rule. Are you ready for this? Over ten years that trainer costs him . . . $62,400! What? Needless to say, he is now working out on his own and taking the free aerobics classes offered at the gym. And honestly he is in better shape than ever.

So what recurring expense can you shock yourself out of?

Grab a Deal When the Market Is Down

I was standing backstage with Donald Trump in Fort Lauderdale on our lecture tour, and he was about to give his two-hour talk to a crowd of thirteen thousand anxious first-time homebuyers and real estate investors. Trump said, putting every other principle of home buying aside, the secret to successful home buying is to do what everyone is *not* doing.

As Trump said to the audience, "Why the hell are you all so upset about a downward market? You should be rejoicing. A bad market is the time to jump in and get a great deal!" Prices are lower, sellers are more motivated, and your meager cash down payment will suddenly have much more buying power.

BYB Tip: Buy When Everyone Else Is Selling

It's Donald Trump's simple yet important rule. When the market is down, it's a great time to jump in. This rule is very simple yet very powerful. It sums up the basic promise of successful home buying and home selling in any market. And this pithy, basic concept comes from one of the most outspoken and successful entrepreneurs of our time.

What You Learned in This Chapter

♦ If you can't afford it, don't buy it.

♦ Calculate how much house you can buy with the money you have. If the numbers don't work out, then you've got two options: (1) Shop for a less expensive property, or (2) Don't buy now—keep saving.

♦ Even if you don't have enough cash right now, build your down payment and boost your buying power using the many ways described in this chapter.

♦ A great way to make your down payment money stretch further is to buy when everyone else is selling. You can buy a lot more house for a lot less cash out of pocket when a market is soft.

CHAPTER 4

Getting Your Credit in Order

The process of buying a house doesn't begin when you walk through the door of your first open house. It needs to begin long before that. So brace yourself. This is big, folks. Buying a house in today's new market is all about your credit and credit scores.

> ### New Rule: Low Credit Scores Lock You Out
>
> Good credit opens the door to success and bad credit will close it. With so many tighter restrictions on lending and mortgages, it is imperative that you have as close to perfect credit and scores as possible. That is why you need to tackle this one immediately.

While writing this book, the news hit that a quarter of Americans have low credit scores (defined as 599 or below), partly due to their spending habits in the past ten years coupled with this recent market downtown and tighter access to credit. On the positive side, the number of consumers who have a top score (800 or above) has increased in recent years. At least in part, this reflects the fact that more individuals have cut spending and paid down debt in response to the recession. Whether your credit is in need of an overhaul or you're looking to preserve your stellar credit, now is the time to address your creditworthiness so you can position yourself to grab the best mortgage at the best rate.

What Your Credit Report Says about You

A credit report is a complete history of all your financial activities. It lists your creditors, when you opened your bank accounts, what you owe and to whom, your credit limits and history—including late payments and any other negative information—your employment history, marriages, divorces, child support history, bankruptcies, property liens, whose name is on what, etc.—it's all there. When lenders request information, this is what they get, and you want to make sure it is in great shape.

Credit Scoring

This process gives a numerical value to all aspects of your credit history, factoring in your income, your debt, and your employment history. The past six to twelve months is examined first, so it's critical to keep current with your bills. Here's how the most popular type of score—the FICO—breaks down:

- 760–850: Acceptable risk. Someone with a score in the high 700s and up to 850, which is a perfect score, is in the best position to get the best interest rates.

- 675–759: Generally acceptable risk and may compensate for other less attractive aspects of your financial past.

- 620–674: Motivates a closer look at potential risks and may inspire a request for credit documentation and letters of explanation.

- 500–619: This lower score may keep the best loans and terms out of reach, as interest rates for these scores are high.

- Below 500: Any score down here falls into the sublender category.

When you go to www.myfico.com and find daily updated mortgage rates on the home page, you'll see that a higher score makes a
real dollar difference. There's also a ton of other important information, starting with tips on how to fix your score.

Obtain Your Credit Report

If you don't have a current one, get your credit report now. If there are
problems, you need to know about them and address them before you
even think about buying. Any serious problems, and sometimes even
minor mistakes, can take months to repair. There are a variety of ways to
get your report. You're entitled to a free credit report once a year under
the FACT Act; just go to www.annualcreditreport.com to retrieve it.
You can also obtain one from each of the three large credit bureaus:

Equifax
www.equifax.com
1-800-685-1111
Equifax Information Services
P.O. Box 740241
Atlanta, GA 30374

Experian
www.experian.com
1-888-397-3742

TransUnion
www.transunion.com
1-800-888-4213
2 Baldwin Place
P.O. Box 1000
Chester, PA 19022

The easiest way to access your report right away is to go online at
the above-mentioned Web sites. You will also want your credit score,
which is the number that reflects your creditworthiness. In addition
to the credit bureaus having their own scoring system, the Fair Isaac
Corporation also puts out scores based on its own formula. Known as

FICO scores, these are also important to obtain because most lenders will look at them as well. In fact, more than 75 percent of all mortgage companies today accept only FICO scores, and 90 percent of the largest U.S. banks use FICO scores. You can go to www.myfico.com and obtain a report from two of the big bureaus and get your FICO scores, too.

Note: we all have three FICO scores—one from each of the three major credit reporting agencies. Experian markets and sells the PLUS Score on its Web site. TransUnion sells the TransRisk score under its TrueCredit brand. Equifax is the only bureau Web site where you can order your FICO score directly; Equifax's score is marketed as Score Power.

I know that all sounds like a bunch of jumble and initials, so to avoid any confusion, I recommend obtaining your FICO scores (from all three bureaus) directly from www.myfico.com.

Clean Up Your Credit Score

Mistakes Happen

Every year a whopping 25 percent of those declined for a mortgage had errors in their credit report. By "errors," I mean inaccuracies in your report. When you spot them, it's up to *you* to fix them. Your credit report will come with information on how to challenge items contained in it that you find false or untrue. You can also find step-by-step guidance at any of the credit bureau sites about filing a claim. Follow the instructions to a T, and keep a good record of your dispute, including copies of any documents you file with the credit bureaus. Once you make an initial claim, you should get a response within thirty to sixty days.

Pay Them Off Waaay Ahead

If you think you can get your credit report cleaned up and ready to go in a matter of days, think again. Even if you have no bad marks on your report and you simply want to make sure all your credit cards are paid up prior to qualifying for a loan, plan way ahead.

I recently wanted to refinance one of my properties. So being the smart, savvy real estate expert that I am, I made sure that I paid off all the credit card bills that I had outstanding ... a few thousand on this one, a couple hundred on that one, a $3,000 balance that I was stupidly owing in my "Checking Plus" bank account.

I sat down with my bank's mortgage agent and confidently told him that I didn't owe anything! All my credit cards and bills were paid off with zero balances. He was impressed.

Cut to ... he pulled up my credit report only to show me that every one of those balances owed was still showing. But I paid them off two months ago, I exclaimed. He believed me, but he said the person doing the calculations to qualify me wouldn't. I had to go home and painstakingly order updated statements from each of the accounts and submit them as well.

The moral of this story: pay it all off waaay ahead, and then lock up your credit cards till your credit score has been checked and you have been approved for your mortgage.

There is also a lot of back-and-forth discussion as to whether you should close accounts that you have paid off. Even though the whole credit rating system seems to be more secretive and convoluted than the final tabulations of the Oscars ... I say just pay off all your credit cards but don't close any of them prior to applying for a mortgage.

Fix Your FICO

The best way to have a good score is to manage your credit responsibly over time.

- Stay current—pay your bills on time.

- Get help—see a credit counselor if you are unable to manage.

- Always make more than the minimum payments on your revolving credit.

- Maintain low balances—pay those balances down!

- Don't move it, lose it—pay off your debt, don't just move it to a new card.

What I have done, and suggest that everyone does, is go to Suze Orman's amazing Web site at www.suzeorman.com. There you will find Suze Orman's FICO Kit. This interactive program allows you to take control of your credit and save money on the interest rates you pay. It really is a great, user-friendly Web site. It has a minimal cost and will be the best investment you can make to get your finances in order.

 BYB Tip: Avoid Credit Repair Scams

For help in finding qualified people who can truly help you to navigate getting your credit in order, be careful. Some services are legitimate, whereas others are not. Do your homework and ask for referrals from friends or family members if you can. Beware of hidden fees, too. You may think that you're paying someone to take the burden of fixing your credit off you, but in reality, you're going to do most of the work. I recommend you start by contacting the National Foundation for Credit Counseling at www.nfcc.org. You can also check out the Federal Trade Commission's Web site at www.ftc.gov for guidance and check up on certain firms through the Better Business Bureau at www.bbb.org.

Worst-Case Credit Scenarios—What Are Your Options?

Yes, in this new market, a great credit score is king. However, when the market was in the height of the market frenzy you would often hear: No Credit—No Problem! Five years ago a monkey with an address and a social security card could get a loan. But it's different now: No Credit—No Way!

Unfortunately for the hundreds of thousands of Americans who got caught in the middle of the market meltdown, there is little chance of getting another mortgage *today*. Tomorrow, however, is another story.

If you are coming out the other end of the financial meat grinder, trying to buy again after walking away or short selling your home, there is some hope.

- **Short Sale Survivors:** If you succumbed to a short sale, according to the new guidelines, you will have to wait approximately two years to qualify for a Freddie Mac or Fannie Mae or FHA loan.

- **Foreclosure Survivors:** If you walked away or went through foreclosure, you will have to wait at least five years to apply for one of the government-backed mortgages.

Many banks, however, may not be quite so forgiving. There may be more of a cooling-off period before they jump back into the mortgage business with you. But that will be up to the individual banks. Just be prepared for a cold shoulder for a while.

 BYB Tip: What if You Don't Have Any Credit?

This will be a hurdle to jump over if, for whatever reason, you lack a credit history or don't have any credit at all. The solution? Start a history now by obtaining a credit card of some sort. If you lack credit because it's been in your spouse's name, then get on the phone and speak with your credit card companies to see what they can do for you. You'll want to have at least one card in your own name. If you must apply for credit, do so. Even if you're the type who pays your bills every month with cash, you can still keep the same habits and pay for your credit card bills in full every month. Having credit doesn't mean you have to actually use your credit. It just means you've been given the responsibility of having access to credit, which is what lenders want to see.

Become the Perfect Buyer—Get Preapproved

Once you have cleaned up your credit scores and know how much money you have to invest, work with a mortgage broker or bank and get a preapproval letter. (I will talk more about selecting the right mortgage broker or bank in chapter 14.) The preapproval letter is your calling card that turns you into the next best thing to a cash buyer because it tells the seller that you are already approved for a mortgage. It is like an all-access pass to the properties in your price range. It telegraphs to a seller that you are not only qualified but prepared and serious about making a deal. You'll want one long before you make an offer because it will make your offer stronger, in either a downward-trending cold or upward-moving hot market.

The Prequalifying Letter—Only a Runner-Up

Not as powerful but still useful is a prequalifying letter. It's an informal albeit professional assessment that basically says you're in good shape financially—but it is nonbinding. It is the result of a lender thoroughly checking out all the financial information you would need to get an actual mortgage, including financial history, credit history, etc. It is also based on a specific mortgage, so do your homework, talk with the lender, and make sure it's the one that you'd want. Always try to get a preapproval letter, but settle for a prequalifying letter if you have to.

What You Learned in This Chapter

♦ The first step to buying a house is to get your credit score perfect by pulling your credit report and addressing problems long before you start house shopping.

♦ Pay down your credit cards waaaaaay ahead of time.

♦ Make sure to check on your FICO scores as well as your credit scores. Banks nowadays will look at both. Find out what yours are and know the difference.

♦ Become the perfect buyer—get a preapproval letter.

CHAPTER 5

The Home You Want

Any good Realtor will tell you that more than half of the battle in the home-buying game is knowing what you want. That may sound simplistic, but it's true. As with anything in life, having a clear picture of the what, where, and how of something you desire makes it easier to attract, locate, and then grab it when the opportunity presents itself.

Before you even begin the process of reviewing potential home candidates—online or at open houses or with your Realtor—you need to think about the features, amenities, room count, size, and type of home you actually need.

Do you want a two-bedroom house with a big backyard? Do you need a three-car garage? How about a condo within walking distance of the train station? Do you want a home to fix up or one that is brand-new?

The House of Your Dreams—Literally

I am a huge believer in the concept that we as individuals can truly create or draw anything we desire into our lives. With focus, attention, thought, and action we can attract things to drop into our laps. I have worked very closely with and lecture-toured with some amazing motivational speakers and life coaches. One in particular, Tony Robbins, has been a powerful influence in my life. I recently toured the country and shared the stage with him, speaking to crowds of ten to fifteen thousand people. He teaches that it's possible to create anything we want as long as we know what "it" is. A house, for example. You can't find that house you want until you have a pretty good picture of what you are looking for.

Let's do an exercise. Sit quietly for a moment and try to imagine your dream house—the one that you want to find and snag for a deal, the one that allows you to be in the neighborhood you'd like to live in today. In your mind's eye, do a walking tour, starting at the curb. Does it have a big front yard? Is it built close to the street? Is it a condo in a modern building? Is it a sprawling gated modern mansion? Or is it an ivy-covered cottage? Is it on the beach or in the mountains? Now open the front door and walk in. Is there a fireplace burning? Are there walls of glass and soaring ceilings, or does the living room look cozy, with beamed ceilings? Next, mentally go to the kitchen, the bedrooms, and all the rest of the rooms until you get to the backyard. Do you hear soft music playing and birds chirping?

Great, now WAKE UP! It's time for a reality check! Unless you have won the lottery, come from a wealthy family, or are buying your second or third home, you are probably not going to be able to purchase your ultimate dream home the first time out. According to Betty Graham of Coldwell Banker in Beverly Hills, many homeowners will own three to four properties before they are able to buy the one they call their dream home.

But you have to start someplace. And putting together your dream house list will help. As I say, you *start* there, because once you have worked through the three steps to house shopping in upcoming chapters, your dream house will be reimagined to a house you can actually afford. In essence, you start with your dream house in mind and trim it back to arrive at an affordable house you can buy today. That way, you can keep your future in sight but dial back to today's realities.

The Dream House Checklist—What Needs to Be on Your List?

The Dream House Checklist comprises six major categories. It helps you organize all the numerous features, elements, and amenities of your new house. There are some that you require and you must have, and there are some that your price may preclude but that you should have. And there are probably some on that checklist that you hadn't even thought about until now.

- ❑ Price
- ❑ Type of property
- ❑ Condition of the house
- ❑ Must-haves and should-haves
- ❑ Location

The Dream House Checklist	
Price	
Type of property	
Condition	
New	
Older/existing	
Mint Condition	
Cosmetic Fixer	
Downright Ugly	
Must-Haves	
Bedrooms	
Bathrooms	
Square footage	
Garage spaces	
Amenities	
Central heating and air	

Kitchen	
Gourmet	
Eat-in	
Outdoor space	
Balcony	
Backyard	
Should-Haves	
Home office space	
How many stories (one floor or two?)	
Architectural style	
Lot size	
Backyard (pool? garden? space to build? space for children to play?)	
Finished basement and/or attic	
Hardwood floors	
Wood-burning fireplace	
Location—Proximity to:	
Job	
Drive—Commute	
Public transportation—Commute	
Walk to work	
Schools	
Shopping	
Entertainment	
Family entertainment	
Singles nightlife	
Recreation	
Nearby freeways	
Walking distance to restaurants	
Low crime rate	
Minimal traffic	

Price

The first qualifier or eliminator, of course, is going to be price. Knowing ahead of time how much you can afford and what you are able to spend immediately enables you to narrow down the vast market of homes to about 10 percent of what's currently on the market. It gives you the ability to focus and select from a much smaller and more easily manageable pool of properties. In terms of finding a price range, once you have a target price you can then give yourself some wiggle room and consider homes within 5 to 10 percent above and below that price. Clearly, 10 percent of a $200,000 house is a lot less money than 10 percent of a $600,000 house. So just be sure that your "range" makes economic sense depending on your numbers and budget.

Type of Property

Are you looking for a traditional house, condo, co-op, or multiunit? And once you decide that, you must consider the pros and cons, the particular benefits and specifics related to each type of property. We'll review these in more detail when we go house shopping in chapter 6, "Older vs. New—Houses vs. Condos—How to Shop Smart for Each."

Condition of Property

New or old? How much sweat equity do you want to put into a property? Do you want to pay a little bit less and invest the time and money it takes to improve the house yourself? Or do you want to buy a house that's brand-new and all you need to bring is your toothbrush? I will put you to the "Hammer Test" in chapter 6.

Must-Haves and Should-Haves

What makes something about a house a "must-have" and another element a "should-have"? Well, the must-have is essential in your new home. For example: "We now have a newborn baby, so we *must* have a two-bedroom house." However, a should-have is not essential and it may get nixed out of the mix if price becomes an issue. For example: "We now have a newborn baby, so we should have a three-bedroom house. That way we can save one room for guests or for a home office." That third bedroom is not a must-have and you could or may have to live with out it to get into a house you can afford.

Square footage is also a must-have. For a first-time house buyer, 1,200 square feet could be a realistic minimum must-have, whereas 2,300 square feet is a should-have. Condo and co-op buyers historically will buy smaller square footages. And of course there are some homebuyers looking for a must-have house of 2,500 square feet with a should-have of 3,500 or more.

And of course a nice clean workable kitchen is a must-have. But a gourmet kitchen with double ovens and Viking stainless steel appliances will be your should-have.

Knowing your must-haves vs. should-haves is a key element to house shopping. It helps both you and your agent to sort through all the properties on the market quickly and easily, helping to focus on the ones that are in your price range and worth your time and energy to view and inspect.

Compromising between Musts and Shoulds

Of course you can and will amend your must-haves and should-haves. As you begin to preview houses, you will have to make some compromises in your list. And separating your musts from your shoulds lets you decide where you can compromise to meet your budget.

You may be pleasantly surprised. For example, you may discover that in your price range and your target neighborhood, you are able to find homes with larger square footage than you originally anticipated. Great. Revise your should-have requirements upward. On the flip, and frustrating side, you may find that you have to manage your expectations a bit. A four-bedroom house with a pool and three-car garage may be out of the realm of possibilities for what you can afford in a given neighborhood. In this case, it's back to your list—time to revise downward. It is right about this time when your dream house becomes your "reality check—what I can afford" dream house!

Matching Your Dream Home to Your Budget—the Starter Home

If you can't make the reality of what you can afford match the houses you are seeing, then you need to remember this doesn't have to be the house you will live in for the rest of your life. The way to match your dream home to your budget is to know that this first house is going to be your starter home.

"Entry-level homes" exist for a reason. You have to accept that the first house or condo you purchase is not going to be the place you'll live in for the rest of your life. But that's okay. Keep in mind that there is no such thing as the "perfect" house. But there is such a thing as a starter home. The good news is that if you buy smart now, you're able to begin the process of gaining equity and appreciation. Coupled with salary increases and smart savings plans, the opportunity to move up exists. When you're ready to move up, this first home can provide you with the funds to purchase your next home or you can even choose to keep it as an investment.

Staying Open-Minded

Yes, you'll need to narrow down your search at some point, but as you begin to play with the choices, keep an open mind. You may be thinking about a house, but there might be a great condo with a cool balcony and view that could be just as fantastic. And in considering conditions of the house or condo, be open to swinging a hammer or getting a bit dirty.

Location

The other significant component of the Dream House Checklist is location. Where do you want to live? By the time most homebuyers have made a decision to buy, they have a basic idea of where they want to live. Proximity to family, friends, and/or work plays a significant part in where a buyer will ultimately want to put down roots. However, within these parameters is a lot of leeway.

In large metropolitan cities like New York City, Boston, Chicago, and San Francisco, mass transportation is readily available and access to numerous residential areas and suburbs is easy. Many people are willing to go where the best value is. Travel a bit outside of the city and you can get more value for your house-buying dollar. That was the original catalyst for the birth of the suburb. Homebuyers in Southern California and metropolitan Atlanta, for instance, have been known to drive well over an hour and a half each way to move to a more affordable community. I know I personally wouldn't do it. I want to spend as little time in the car commuting between the studio and home as possible.

Selecting Your Dream Neighborhood

To be successful in your quest to find the perfect neighborhood, you have to invest time in the process. It's actually the very same process you just went through when you refined your dream house checklist. And just like in that process, you have to analyze your must-haves and should-haves for the perfect dream location.

Got an hour or two, or a free afternoon? Get out and drive around and explore neighborhoods in your community. That's the only way you'll get to check out the hoods with which you are unfamiliar. Think of it as research on four wheels. The old adage to "buy the worst house on the best block" still rings true, but the trick is to find the best block for you!

Balancing Price and Location

You now are pretty clear about how much you can afford and the price range you need to consider. Now comes the major tug-of-war ... between where you want to live and what you can actually afford.

Sure, we all want to live in the swankiest part of town. But your budget may not support that choice. In some metro areas that $300,000 price may only buy you a small condo in the city, a fixer-upper in a less desirable part of town, or a nicer, newer house out in the burbs.

Be prepared for this price versus location battle. I warn you, it could get ugly. But my advice on this is to stay very strict on your price limitations. Don't overspend. Adjust your location should-haves before you even consider adjusting your must-have target price. You can live in a slightly less desirable neighborhood, but you can't live in a house you can't afford!

Getting More House for Your Money— Neighborhoods on the Rise

One of the best ways to stretch your buying dollar is to find a neighborhood that is in transition. Called fringe or transitional neighborhoods, they are typically close to major metropolitan areas and were once neglected and less desirable. Is there a trendy restaurant where a tattoo parlor used to be? These neighborhoods are now beginning to enjoy a new life, and your goal is to find them.

Buying in a transitional neighborhood for your first house allows you to get into the market relatively cheaply and build some equity. Your house gains value as the neighborhood improves. It may not be your dream location, or the seaside beach community you want to retire to, but as I've said, over time you will build even more equity and then move on at some point.

 BYB Tip: Wake Up and Smell the Coffee

Has a Starbucks just opened on the corner or maybe a Whole Foods Market? These are all good signs that a neighborhood is on the upswing. You can bet that big chains like Starbucks spend a lot of money and time analyzing neighborhood potential before they open up a new store. So go ahead, tap into their market research and be their neighbor.

Factoring in the Commute—a Major Location Consideration

Ah . . . the American Dream: a three-bedroom home in the suburbs. Argh . . . the American nightmare: an hour and a half drive to work! If you have the kind of job that punches the clock every day and puts you on the nine-to-five work schedule, this whole commuting thing is an enormous factor in deciding where you are going to buy. You need to consider the pros and cons of a long commute, walking to work, and everything in between.

 BYB Buyer's Blunder: Not Counting the Commute

Neglecting to consider the cost of commuting when selecting a neighborhood and a house is foolish. This happens to be one of the items homebuyers most often forget to add into their monthly budgets. They often fail to take into account the impact of commuting on their quality of life as well.

Adding Up the Cost of Commuting

- **Cost of gas**—Let's do the math to see how much every month you would spend on gas if, for example, you commuted forty miles each way to work, five days a week. If you got twenty miles per gallon and paid $3.25 a gallon, that comes out to $260 a month, or $3,120 per year just for the gas!

- **Wear and tear on your car**—Now include the cost of the wear and tear of those 1,600 miles a month, or 19,200 miles per year, on your car. That could be worth thousands in repairs and decreased life span of your car. Wow.

- **What is your time worth?**—This expense is one that speaks for itself. It's one of those intangible costs that they talk about in the Visa commercials—priceless.

If you factor that extra money into your monthly budget, the slightly less expensive house farther from your job may not really be less expensive. You had better check. But keep in mind that even after you run the numbers and factor in the commuting costs you still may be getting much more home for your money and a lot more of your must-haves and should-haves. I just want to make sure that you don't forget to add these costs in when making the decision and also planning for your monthly ongoing expenses.

Moving In Ahead of Time

Okay, I'm not suggesting you pitch a tent in the backyard of your prospective new house and consider yourself moved in. I just mean you should pretend to . . . at least for one or two mornings. Show up at your potential new neighborhood at 7:30 in the morning and pretend you're going into work. Test the commute during a morning rush hour. No cheating here—not on a Sunday afternoon. It's crucial to find out what your commute time is really going to be during commute time.

Ultimately, nobody wants to spend hours on the road. And the actual distance is not a true indicator of your commuting time. A really great example of this is in major metropolitan cities. In Los Angeles, you can live in a lovely section of town called Hancock Park. It's only ten miles from a business hub in Santa Monica. But during rush hour it can take as much as an hour and fifteen minutes to get between the two points. So don't get stuck in a home that may be "so close and yet so far."

 BYB Tip: Commute Online

Once you have spotted a house or neighborhood, determine your distance to work, your mother-in-law's house, your child's day care center, whatever you like. Just go to www.mapquest.com or www .google.com/maps and enter the house address and the target address. Bang—there it is: the mileage from your new home base. But again, remember—distance online or on paper does not take traffic into consideration!

Lifestyle Dictates Location

You need to keep in mind that lifestyle is a big factor in choosing a location. Are you single or raising a family? Are you retiring and downsizing? Where you are in your life makes a difference in where you'll be happy living.

If you are married and raising a family, access to great schools, family parks, neighborhoods with big backyards, and places for children to play are going to be your priority. Safety and security are big factors as well.

Retirees are going to want to locate in areas that have great public transportation, lots of other retired people, good doctors, hospitals, organized social activities, and recreation.

Single Homebuyers

Home-buying trends have changed over the last decade and in today's new market more single homebuyers are entering the real estate market than ever before. Single women have now outpaced single men as a percentage of homebuyers. A whopping 21 percent of all new home purchases are credited to single women. But as far as must-haves, what do singles tend to look for? A single man or woman or newly married couple wants to be closer to where the action is—great restaurants, nightlife, theaters, movies, sporting events, shopping, etc.

Tips for Single Buyers

1. **Stay within your budget**—Buying a home on your own is a fantastic move and great step toward your financial future. But make sure it's a home you can afford if there is a momentary—or longer—blip in your financial profile. If you lose a job, you have a health issue, or anything else happens that could affect your ability to cover your monthly costs, remember you don't have a spouse or significant other to fall back on for the additional monthly nut. So while you are on your own, don't overextend. Buy a home well within your means.

2. **Guess who's gonna mow the grass**—Being the only person with a set of house keys also means being the only person responsible for maintenance. A leaky faucet and overgrown lawn won't take care of themselves. For those single homebuyers who find the idea of maintaining a yard a bit daunting, or who worry that climbing up ladders to clean out the gutters every rainy season is just too "hands-on" for them, condominiums

and townhomes or even smaller homes in new communities require less exterior maintenance and might be a good option. In other words, don't buy a home you can't manage yourself.

3. **Look out for your safety and security**—Remember that being a single homeowner doesn't allow for someone to be home the majority of the time. So you will need to consider safety and security issues. You want to be able to lock the door on your way out, and not have to think twice about it. So make sure you are in a low-crime neighborhood and the house or condo feels safe and secure.

4. **Consider resale value and longevity**—Purchasing a home is a great long-term investment. However, there are many reasons single homebuyers may need to move, such as relocating for a job or a lifestyle change. Therefore, it's important to think about the resale value of prospective properties during the search. You want to be aware of homes and condos that have great general appeal and will be easy to resell if need be.

5. **Keep an eye on the future**—You buy yourself a nice little home or condo now. But someday you might not be single and you'll add a significant other to your team and possibly even children. Though additional space may not be needed immediately, it's important to consider potential future plans for a home. Having a spare bedroom, if it's affordable, is a smart choice.

Single homebuyer bonus: You Just Got Hotter—How fantastic that you, a single man or woman, are already planning to be a homeowner. Being financially smart and responsible may have seemed like strictly your parents' lifestyle a decade ago. It used to be sexy to be footloose and fancy-free, spending all your income on living the high life. Well, when the economy turned in 2007, that disposable-cash lifestyle became just that—disposable. So don't think that if you are a single gal with your own home, men will find that intimidating. And don't think that if you are a single guy with your own home, women will think you are too set in your ways. Being a smart and financially responsible homeowner is the new sexy! That's right, you just became hotter.

New Rule: Less Is More. Think Small.

According to Stephen Gandel, senior writer at *Time* magazine, when it comes to buying a home, think smaller. Less is more. In this new economy and today's new market, downsizing is in vogue. Smaller houses, no more than three bedrooms and two or three baths, are also going to be a commodity in the coming years. As population patterns shift, and as the baby boomers downsize, there is going to be a great demand for smaller homes. Those five- and six-bedroom McMansions are not as popular as they used to be. They are more costly to maintain, you are paying for space you may never use, and they are harder to resell. Smaller homes are more practical and affordable, and their value will continue to climb as the demand becomes greater.

What You Learned in This Chapter

- Before you begin shopping for real, you need to create a Dream House Checklist that specifies: price, type of property, condition of the house, must-haves, should-haves, and location.

- You will most likely have to make compromises. Your dream house will become your "reality check—what I can afford" dream house.

- Must-haves are your bottom-line house requirements. Should-haves are items that you might have to give up to keep your house in your price range.

- Price versus location is always a tug-of-war.

- Seek out neighborhoods on the rise to help you find a house to fit your budget.

- Make sure to include the cost of commuting into your monthly budget and consider the pros and cons on your lifestyle.

PART THREE

Smart Shopping

CHAPTER 6

Older vs. New—Houses vs. Condos— How to Shop Smart for Each

Older homes, new condos, co-ops, older condos, newly constructed houses, preconstruction homes, or multiunits with income potential. So many choices. Each property has pros and cons. And each property has a unique set of shopping rules. There are so many factors to consider. Older homes have charm but need work, new homes may lack a community neighborhood feeling but have great new bells and whistles. Condos are often located right in the heart of all the best restaurants and near transportation but lack any outdoor space to garden and feel close to nature.

It's important to learn the differences and how to shop smartly so you know to spot a good one when you find it.

- Older/existing/fixer home

- New construction/preconstruction

- Condo

- Co-op

- Duplex/triplex

Should you buy new or old? House or condo? The answers to these questions aren't clear-cut because so much can factor in, such as price, affordability, availability, your personal preferences, location, lifestyle, and your other must-haves and should-haves.

Let me tell you about my friend Bruno. He started out looking at older homes. He was really committed to finding the type of home that he grew up in—a '70s-style ranch that needed a little TLC. Well, then he started to look at new construction. When he walked into the first model home on a preconstruction site, his mouth dropped and his heart literally skipped a beat. He was instantly enamored of the shiny new appliances, the freshly painted walls, and the granite countertops. He had to have new construction.

However, after taking a step back—pushing his emotions aside and leaning more toward his intellect—he realized that the flashy new house had great square footage but . . . wait . . . something was missing. A backyard! Yes, all the homes in the development were built so close together, there was nothing more than a wood deck that faced the back of the neighbor's house—a spitting distance away. And on further inspection, there was barely a front yard. The houses were so tight to the street that there was nary a patch of lawn to mow!

It was at this point that Bruno decided to turn his attention back to an older home—a fixer was the way to go for him. He realized that to match his Dream House Checklist must-haves, he needed a backyard where he could install a swing between two trees and gently rock away his worries. And that wasn't going to happen in a new-construction tract of homes.

On the other hand, a colleague, David, had the opposite experience. He and his wife, Sheila, lived in Philadelphia. He and Sheila headed to Ft. Lauderdale to look for a nice small house that was near the beach. They saw lots of cute Floridian houses with pools. But one day while having lunch at a lovely beachside café they looked up to see a For Sale sign. It was in front of a relatively new condo right at the beach and well within their price range, and it hit almost all of their dream house must-haves. They sought a home that would be easy to maintain and keep safe and secure as they traveled back and forth to Pennsylvania. But it turned out that condo living rather than a beachside house was for them, and they couldn't be happier.

Older/Existing/Fixer Homes

I want to begin the discussion of the different types of properties by reviewing older homes. They constitute the largest category of home sales in the United States, so chances are very good that you will consider this category either now or at some point in the future.

Any home or condo that has been "lived in" is considered an older home. The real estate industry calls older homes "existing" homes, or even fixers if they need a little extra TLC. So you will see me jump back and forth throughout the book referencing both older and existing homes. But know that they mean the same thing.

Older/Existing/Fixer Homes—the Pros

Ah, the charm, the detail, the attention to architectural style. A '20s Craftsman, a '40s cottage, a '50s postwar, a '60s ranch style, a '70s split level ... and my personal favorite ... the midcentury modern. Here are the pluses to these gems:

- They've got more charm. The older a home is, the more likely it is to have architectural details and decorative elements that give it personality that you rarely find in new construction.

- There's more selection. There are more of these homes than in any of the other categories of homes. More to choose from means more opportunities to find what you want and better bargaining power for the buyer.

- They're a bit more spacious than today's cookie-cutter new construction.

- The older home usually sits on a larger piece of land.

- The older home is usually located in a more developed and established community. I grew up, for example, in the small town of Collingswood, New Jersey. You could walk or ride your bike to the main street with lots of shops and stores. I've personally never liked living in a new, gated community. I like the established town feeling.

- They're frequently less expensive. Often an existing home is more affordable.

- You have the opportunity to add value to your home with renovation. Upgrades allow for a degree of personal satisfaction, and you can tailor the home to your specific taste.

- With a fixer-upper, you're not paying for someone else's improvements.

Older/Existing/Fixer Homes—the Cons

Yep, there are lots of reasons to buy an older home, but along with the pluses comes a list of minuses. Older homes are rarely move-in ready. Well, some are. But most have varying degrees of needed repairs, upgrades, and renovations. And by the nature of the terminology, fixers are never bring-in-your-furniture-and-toothbrush-ready. To be fair to those of you who are hammer and screwdriver challenged, and not willing to get your hands dirty or face the demands of fixing up a property, take note:

- They can sometimes require lots of renovations, which, of course, requires lots of money.

- For first-time buyers, dishing out the down payment is enough to break the bank. Coming up with the extra cash to bring the house up to your speed designwise may be very difficult.

- The renovation process can be painful to endure and very unsettling if you are not ready for the challenge.

- Your house will be messy and perhaps unlivable for an uncertain time period.

- You may have to relocate temporarily and not be sure when you can move back in because you can't figure out how long it will take, despite the promises from the contractor.

- You never really know how much it will all end up costing. My rule of renovation is that it will always cost you 20 percent more than you planned.

- Such a chaotic experience can oftentimes wreak havoc on the best of relationships.

Fixer-Uppers Are Money in Your Pocket!

A significant portion of existing homes are what I call fixer-uppers. I love these properties, especially ones I can restore back to their original architectural style and glory. I have bought and restored many early 1900s Craftsman homes, some 1920s Spanish-style houses, and numerous amazing 1950s and '60s midcentury homes. With a little TLC, some hard work, and sweat equity, you can turn a real dog of a fixer into a gorgeous dream home . . . and build a lot of e-q-u-i-t-y in the process.

This is one of my favorite midcentury makeovers—what I would call a "Downright Ugly" house.

Amazing how an architectural house with great bones can be transformed into a beautiful home.

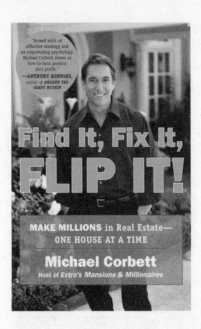

I am a huge proponent of buying a fixer, improving it, adding value to it, and then eventually selling it for a profit.

I could go on for chapters about how a little sweat equity, and knowledge about which improvements to make, can add enormous value to your home and set you on the road to eventual financial independence. But I won't! You will have to go to my Web site, MichaelCorbett.com, or just buy a copy of my first bestselling book, *Find It, Fix It, Flip It! Make Millions in Real Estate—One House at a Time.*

But seriously, this chapter is going to give you a great overview of how to spot the older home or fixer with the right things wrong, how to tell the fixers apart, and how to know what improvements are the big equity builders.

So, as you read through this chapter and make your decisions about older versus new, and homes versus condos, you know I vote for the older fixers!

Four Categories of Older/Existing/Fixer Homes

If you have decided that an older home, an older condo, or even an older multiunit is for you, then your next step is to decide what level of challenge you are ready to tackle. Not all older homes require the same level of redo, renovation, and fixing up. In fact, there are actually four categories of older/existing/fixer properties. You'll want to decide what you are personally comfortable with and able to manage. In other words, do you want an older home that is in perfect condition or one that needs a little—or even a lot of—work?

Are You Handy with a Hammer?

How do you know which category of older home is right for you? Well, older homes will generally fit into one of four major categories, each one based on how much muscle you'll have to put into making it perfect.

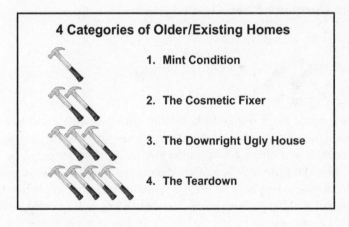

4 Categories of Older/Existing Homes

1. **Mint Condition**

2. **The Cosmetic Fixer**

3. **The Downright Ugly House**

4. **The Teardown**

Mint Condition

It's done, it's perfect, it's move-in condition, it's blue ribbon ready. This house is generally one that someone else has renovated and updated. You won't have to do much at all except arrange your furniture and use that hammer to hang a few mirrors.

The only thing to keep in mind is you will pay top dollar, even in a bad market, for this house because you are paying for someone else's sweat equity and hard work. But it's okay to buy in this category if you have decided that you don't want to run all over town selecting just the right kitchen faucet and matching-finish door handles. That is why this house has got a one-hammer rating.

The Cosmetic Fixer

A Cosmetic Fixer is a good house for someone who wants to buy, spruce up, and stay for a while. It is the house that just needs a bit of cleanup. It gets only a two-hammer level of difficulty rating.

The sale price will be slightly discounted from the Mint Condition version. The purchase price is going to be only a bit below the full market value because sellers and their Realtors know that with a little bit of paint and a trip or two to the home improvement store, these cosmetic fixers are as good as new.

You will find that this Cosmetic Fixer has most of its systems intact. Meaning newer roof, newer heating and air, copper plumbing, updated electrical. All the things to which your inspector will give a general thumbs-up, once you have put in an offer.

The Cosmetic Fixer is the reason you will spend many weekends at your local home improvement center. There you will be picking paint, entertaining fresh landscaping, maybe considering some new lighting fixtures, buying wall-to-wall carpeting, and choosing some new appliances.

The Downright Ugly House

This is the house of your handyman dreams! It needs more extensive fix-it work than the Cosmetic Fixer. This is the house that, when renovated, will give you the best long-term value increase for your dollar. By the way, I call this the Downright Ugly house because when someone steps out of the car to look at this house they will usually exclaim, "Well, *that* is just downright ugly!"

Here are some qualities that will give you an idea of what "downright ugly" means to me.

Exterior

- No current curb appeal (ugly, run-down—pick one) but lots of potential

- Great bones—good construction and architectural lines that have been underutilized or not accentuated

- Little or no landscape—my personal favorite

- A few minor structural problems, e.g., a sagging foundation

- Abandoned car in the driveway—always a big plus!

Interior

- Dark interiors cloaked in drapery and blinds—a turnoff for other buyers

- Upgrades needed in the house systems—electrical, plumbing, heating, air

- Extremely dated kitchens and barely functioning bathrooms

- Rotting subfloors in the kitchen or bathroom

- Evidence of pets—bad smells aplenty

- Leaks in the roof and a water-stained ceiling

- Lots of small rooms, creating a chopped-up, claustrophobic feeling

Why the Downright Ugly Is Beautiful to You

This house is a diamond in the rough. If you can see through all that ugly, you'll get the deal that others miss. It requires vision and a leap of faith. Trust me, every time I buy a Downright Ugly house, I still think, "What have I done?" But, in addition to having lots of sweat equity potential, this house is going to come with a very nice reduced price tag. Thus in a sense you are making money when you buy the Downright Ugly house, as well as when you fix it up and eventually sell it.

The wonderful advantage of buying a Downright Ugly house is that you have the opportunity to add value to it. That way, you are building instant equity and not paying top dollar for someone else's improvements . . . pretty good reasons to strap on that tool belt.

 BYB Tip: Downright Ugly Success Story

One of my best home bargains was a Downright Ugly house I spotted that had been sitting on the market for quite some time. This house's front wall had sunk to one side. Even the front door wouldn't open. Many unknowledgeable buyers tried to push through that crooked door and went running back out to their cars. I, however, called a foundation expert and got an estimate for the work prior to making the offer. He quoted me only $2,000. Yet I made an offer that was $50,000 below the asking price of $400,000. I got the house at $350,000. Moral of the story? What looked to be a three-hammer project turned out to be a two-hammer no-brainer.

The Teardown—What It Is and Why You Don't Want It

The Teardown is the house with "broken bones"; it is the money pit you must run from. It's a house with the wrong things wrong. By that I mean the house has *major* structural, geological, foundational, or environmental problems. You don't want it. Even if you get the house cheap . . . really cheap. The problems never go away and are sometimes impossible to fix no matter how much money you throw at them.

Besides the expense, you'll often need architectural plans drawn up, full permits, and approval from the city inspectors for every stage of repairs. And these major structural flaws are sometimes covering up other underlying and costly issues. Often, it is not sufficient just to repair these problems. With significant repairs, you will have to bring the entire house up to current codes, which on an older home could run into the tens of thousands of dollars. This is a Pandora's box you do not want to open.

Red-Flag Reasons Not to Buy a House

Structural Problems That Are Beyond Repair Economically

- Foundations that are inferior or not built on slab or concrete footings

- Major shifting due to poor foundation work

- Unsolvable drainage issues and flooding of the basement

- A bad floor plan that can only be solved by a room addition

- Bedrooms on the second floor with no bathrooms and no room to add one

- Major truss damage to the roof, causing a severely sagging roof line

- Major fire damage

- Illegal room additions that are not to code, especially bathrooms

Geological Problems That You Cannot Overcome

- Severe earthquake damage

- Unstable hillside near the house

- Slipping or shifting due to soil erosion or flooding

- A house built on soil compaction—substandard by today's codes

Environmental Problems to Run From

- Asbestos ducting

- Mold

- An old, outdated septic system

- Faulty septic system or a long sewer line to the street

- High levels of radon

Estimate Repair Costs before You Make an Offer

Can you really estimate your fix-it or improvement costs before you make an offer? Not only can you, but you are going to have to if you want to accurately assess a home's true worth in its current condition. But don't worry, right off the bat I'm going to say that making that first ballpark estimate is not easy. But you are going to get some help here.

Put Together Your Fix-It Hit List

Once you have targeted a potential fixer home, you will need to identify as best as you can all potential fix-it projects and organize them using the Fix-It Hit List. I have put together a Fix-It Hit List for you to use for every potential house you review. You'll find it as well as on my Web site, at www.MichaelCorbett.com; or go to www.Coldwell Banker.com/BeforeYouBuy to download for free.

Your Fix-It Hit List will be your bible. Carry it with you every time you look at a house. Refer to it. It's like having the answers to the test. As you are shopping, you don't need to have the answers to every single item on this list. But it sure helps to have this list with you as you house shop. Believe me, by the time you look at your third or fourth house you will not remember which one had the leaky roof, which one had the missing floorboards, or which one had the bad added-on porch. This list keeps track of the notable repairs and allows you to make notes about how much your repair and fix-it costs might be.

The Fix-It Hit List			
Address _____ Description: Style _____ Bedrooms _____ Baths _____ Square Footage _____ Age _____ Garage _____ Attached _____ Detached _____			
Item	**Good**	**Repair**	**Add/ Replace**
SYSTEMS			
Electrical System			
Panel			
Amperage			
Age of panel			
Plumbing			
Main line			
Sewage line			
Septic tank			
Main line clean-out			
Copper lines			
Hot-water heater			

Item	Good	Repair	Add/ Replace
Heating and Cooling			
Central air			
Forced air			
Heating and air			
Foundation			
Bolting			
Re-supporting			
Cement slab			
INTERIOR			
Kitchen			
Plumbing			
Sink			
Faucets			
Garbage disposal			
Soap dispensers			
Countertops			
Cabinets			
Hardware			
Appliances			
Refrigerator			
Oven			
Cooktop			
Dishwasher			
Freezer			
Hood			
Ice-maker			
Microwave			
Trash compactor			
Electrical			
Lighting			

Item	Good	Repair	Add/ Replace
Under-counter lights			
GFIs			
Outlets			
Switches/dimmers			
Flooring			
Carpet			
Vinyl			
Tile			
Hardwood			
Subfloor			
Windows			
Skylight			
Master Bath			
Vanity/Cabinets			
Countertops			
Plumbing			
Sink			
Shower pans			
Shower head			
Bathtub			
Jacuzzi			
Toilet			
Bathtub enclosure			
Shower doors			
Wall tile			
Floor tile			
Repair subfloor			
Accessories (towel racks, etc.)			
Medicine cabinet			

Item	Good	Repair	Add/Replace
Electrical			
GFIs			
Switches/dimmers			
Light fixtures			
Mirrors			
Windows			
Bathroom 2			
Vanity/Cabinets			
Countertops			
Plumbing			
Sink			
Shower pans			
Shower head			
Bathtub			
Jacuzzi			
Toilet			
Bathtub enclosure			
Shower doors			
Wall tile			
Floor tile			
Repair subfloor			
Accessories (towel racks, etc.)			
Medicine cabinet			
Electrical			
GFIs			
Switches/dimmers			
Light fixtures			
Mirrors			
Windows			
Walls			
Ceilings			

Item	Room	Hallways	Add/Replace
Powder Room			
Sink			
Cabinet/Pedestal			
Toilet			
Electrical			
Lighting			
GFIs			
Accessories			
Tiling			
Flooring			
Living Room, Dining Room, Den, Hallways			
Fireplace mantel			
Electrical			
Lighting fixtures			
Recessed lighting			
Outlets			
Dimmers			
Skylights			
Light fixtures			
Crown molding			
Windows			
Flooring			
Hardwood			
Tile			
Carpet			
Master Bedroom			
Flooring			
Hardwood			
Carpet			
Lighting			

Item	Room	Hallways	Add/ Replace
Closet organizer			
Bedrooms			
Flooring			
Hardwood			
Carpet			
Lighting			
Closet organizer			
Laundry			
Plumbing			
Sink			
Faucet			
Cabinets			
Countertops			
Washer/Dryer			
Laundry chute			
Attic			
Insulation			
Structural reinforcement			
Vents			
Basement			
Sump pump			
Windows			
Moisture issues			
Lighting			
Storage/Shelving			
EXTERIOR			
Exterior General			
Roof			

Item	Room	Hallways	Add/ Replace
Gutters			
Chimney			
Aluminum siding			
Stucco walls			
Wood siding			
Windows			
Screens			
Exterior doors			
French			
Sliding			
Glass			
Wood			
Pool			
Spa			
Front door			
Mailbox			
House numbers			
Front porch			
Landscape			
Sprinkler system			
Trees			
Shrubs			
Lawn			
Hedging			
Fences			
Site drainage			
Hardscape			
Driveway			
Pathways			
Decks			

Item	Room	Hallways	Add/ Replace
Patios			
Stone paving			
Brick paving			
Masonry			
Garage			
Garage doors			
Shelving			
Interior Painting			
Walls			
Ceilings			
Interior doors			
Woodwork			
Exterior Painting			
Walls			
Masonry			
Siding			
Woodwork			

A Little Repair Advice, Please

When it comes to advice and guidance on repair and renovation sources, your Realtor is once again invaluable. Chances are he or she has sold numerous houses in your potential neighborhood. Your Realtor can help you network with the dozens of homebuyers and sellers her or she has worked with, people who may have lists of good tradesmen and contractors they would be willing to recommend. Another resource to take advantage of is the Realtor's concierge service. For example, Coldwell Banker offers its buyers across the country a full roster of contractor and tradesman references. This is a real benefit when buying your first fix-it house. A concierge service will present you with three to four referrals in any category of workman you require, all of whom have been scrutinized by the local realty office. These tradesmen:

- Are licensed and bonded.

- Have references.

- Are motivated to make you happy—because if there is a problem, they may well lose their referral.

Home Improvement Centers

Big chain stores like Lowe's are full of materials you will need, fixtures you will install, and ideas you can use. Expect to spend many hours at these places. When buying a Downright Ugly house, you'll be there so often, they'll be giving you a parking place with your name on it.

Lowe's provides free design service and also installation experts who will literally design your kitchens and bathrooms right before your eyes. Once you approve the design and work with them to select materials and colors, they arrive at your home to install it all. It is a first-time homeowner's dream. It takes the fear out of fixers.

Whatever you're looking for is in these stores in some form or another. You can comparison shop for everything from parquet flooring to countertops and from windows to washers. Go. Ask. Write things down. Go back. Ask more questions or go to www.lowes.com/home101.

Weekend Home Improvement Conventions and Home Shows

Held several times a year at convention centers in most major cities and advertised in the local papers, home shows are a great source of information in one place. With hundreds of vendors, the latest technologies, and helpful salespeople to answer questions, you can get ideas and learn about new services.

Help on the Internet

Another great resource for home repairs, estimates, contractors, and tradesman is the Internet. There are sites out there that will actually recommend individual service providers, and give customer ratings for each, but you have to be careful. Some are more reliable than others. My personal favorite is Angie's List, started in 1995 (www.angies list.com). The site is a fantastic resource for first-time homebuyers, novice renovators, and veteran home remodelers alike, giving members access to local skilled and qualified workers, as defined by other consumers who have used their services already. One of the things I like about this site is that the founder, Angie Hicks, doesn't allow anonymous reviews, saying, "I think people should stand behind their praise or criticism of a service company, and we've always held our members accountable for accurate reporting."

 BYB Tip: Need More Square Footage? Keep Looking

Avoid houses that need room additions. I never add square footage beyond the actual footprint or roofline of the house. It is just too time-consuming, and the permitting process and the architectural plans and engineering involved are just too overwhelming for first-time homebuyers . . . or even second- or third-time homebuyers with a bit of renovation expertise under their belts. If you are looking for a house with more square footage or that extra room, don't plan to add on. Just keep looking.

 BYB Tip: The Corner Lot

I am not a big fan of the house on the corner. My grandma's house in Collingswood, New Jersey, was on the corner. It had lots of land, but most of it was streetside and not really all that usable. Plus, you have traffic on two sides of your home, not just one. It's a bit more exposed than a house in the middle of the block. And a corner lot is a little harder to make secure, especially if you have kids that you want to keep an eye on at playtime.

BYB Tip: A Little Charm Can Be a Very Good Thing

The more architectural detail a house already has, the easier and less expensive it is to create charm. It's already there: all you have to do is showcase it. For the smaller house, look for details that you can accentuate. With an older house keep some of the elements, like the original tiles and maybe even some of the original cabinets. Just dress them up with new hardware. Classic architectural styles like Craftsman, turn of the century, and cottage are loaded with architectural detail. Keep the old bathroom fixtures as well, even if you upgrade the plumbing and electrical throughout. It's a money saver and creates a classic look.

New and Preconstruction Houses and Condos

Okay, now that you've got a good overview of the older/existing/ fixer house, let's examine the new and preconstruction house and condo route. Hundreds of thousands of new homes and condos have been built in the past ten years nationwide. At this point there is a surplus of them, so in today's new market there are some good deals to be had . . . and some land mines to avoid.

The Pros

- You are moving into a house that should be completed and perfect and have that "new house smell."

- With new construction or preconstruction purchases, the work is done for you. You don't have to do a darn thing. You don't have to lift a finger, or a hammer.

- Okay, yes, maybe make a few decisions about what color to paint the breakfast room or if you want the white or the stainless steel appliances—that is, the fun stuff. A big financial benefit to a new home is that you won't have much maintenance to do for quite a while. With brand-new appliances, plumbing, heating, and air, you should be repair free for a few years.

- They come with some of the amenities that today's lifestyle demands—open, eat-in kitchens; walk-in closets; large master baths.

- New homes and condos are often equipped with the latest technology built right in—alarm systems, speaker systems, Internet wiring, and cable.

The Cons

- They can cost more than existing homes.

- They can entail living in new neighborhoods built far from necessary destinations, like supermarkets, schools, and shopping centers.

- They may not excite someone who wants to do lots of customizing and upgrading. People who take pleasure in fixing up a home and tailoring it to their preferences may not find brand-new homes suitable.

- Oftentimes new homes and condos have less architectural detail and charm.

- New home lot sizes are smaller than older homes. If you are looking for that big backyard, you may not find it.

Seven Land Mines in New and Preconstruction House Shopping

1. Empty Lots = Empty Promises

Yes, there are great deals out there right now, but today's market has brought forward a whole new list of *caveat emptors*, or "buyer-bewares." Brand-new homes in huge developments outside of downtown Las Vegas have sold at fire-sale prices.

I've driven into many developments in which only twenty of the forty lots have houses already built. The other twenty lots are giant plots of dirt that kick up sand and dust the moment the wind picks up. This is not your ideal neighborhood. And though it may seem like a very good deal to you now, it will become very difficult to resell the house sitting next to twenty empty lots in a half-finished community.

⚠️ **BYB Buyer's Blunder: Buying into Half-Finished Developments**

There are lots of buildings and developments out there that have sat half empty. Many tract developments of homes remain half completed. Be warned, even though you may be getting a great deal you may be buying into a development or community that may never be fully completed—or that may take too long to come back to life. You'll be stuck with an unsellable house in the middle of an unfinished community.

Yes, the developers will promise to finish the development and say that all the lots are sold, but judging from their track record I use the phrase "empty lots = empty promises" as an adage to house shop by.

2. You Are Not Just Buying a House—You're Buying a Developer

Big new developments and newly constructed gated communities can fail before they are completed and leave you holding a devalued home. For example, if you buy a new home that's not done yet, or hasn't even been started, you are also buying a developer. What if he runs out of money before he's done? This is why it's important to do your homework on any developer when you are considering a purchase. Better to go with well-known companies that have a history of successful developments than to say yes to a newbie who won't let you see his financials. Check with current homeowners in the development and see if their homes have retained their value and if they have any serious complaints.

3. Don't Be Fooled by Models—Know Their Tricks of the Trade!

When buying new construction generally you don't ever get to see your actual home or unit. You see a model or prototype that is similar in floor plan to the home or apartment you are purchasing. Those model homes are always decorated and dressed to look magnificent and perfectly showcase that fabulous lifestyle you will instantly have the moment you purchase this home. However, buyer beware! There are lots of tricks to the trade when it comes to dressing model homes.

The developers and designers employ all kinds of techniques to make the model appear bigger than it actually is. Oftentimes they are furnished and staged with slightly smaller-scale furnishings to make the rooms look bigger. Bedrooms generally have double-sized mattresses rather than traditional queens or kings.

So just as in real life, the same holds true for house shopping . . . don't be distracted by model looks.

 BYB Tip: Something's Missing

One of the sneakiest tricks of all is removing many of the interior doors between rooms to give the model home a much greater feeling of space and flow. Don't let that door trick slam you in the . . . face!

4. Extras and Upgrades

What's extra? Find out exactly which upgrades are—and are not—included in the price you are being quoted. Wow, this place is a steal: it's only $300,000 for a four-bedroom house just outside of Philadelphia. What you didn't think to ask was if the finished basement and the gourmet kitchen package are included.

 BYB Tip: Don't Go on an Upgrade Shopping Spree

Be conservative about which and how many upgrades you select. Determine which extras and upgrades you can live without or do on your own later. Just as with any retail business, builders make their biggest markups and profits on the upgrades.

5. When's It Going to Be Finished?

What is the date of completion of the building? Does it coincide with your needs? And is there a cancellation clause or a refund of deposit clause if the builder does not complete the house, building, or development by a specified promise date?

6. The Multiple Phases of Buying in a New Development

Looking at the new homes in phase 2 of a development? Go back to phase 1. If you are buying in a community that is a phase 2 or higher, then hit up some neighbors in phase 1. How was this developer to deal with? Any suggestions? Advice?

Are you looking at an existing subdivision or tract home community where building is still taking place? Is the developer already working on the next phase? Here's some special advice:

■ If you are looking at an existing home in phase 1, head over to phase 2 and check out the competition. You might be able to get a better deal from the seller if the market has softened and phase 2 is selling for less than the existing house in phase 1.

■ If you are looking for new construction and you are previewing homes in phase 2, you may want to head back over to the phase 1 homes and see if there are any bargains on the market. In addition, the phase 1 neighborhood is already established, with grown-in landscaping and completed, lovely homes. You might just prefer that to a new phase surrounded by bulldozers, infant trees, and blowing dust.

 BYB Tip: New Construction Gone Wrong

Quick story here. I bought a home in Palm Springs, California. It was under construction. But more important, the house sat on the sixth tee of a golf course that was also under construction. I am a pretty smart guy but sometimes too trusting. I specifically asked the Realtor who was selling the property for the builder, "Where is the golf cart path going to be? Right on the other side of my property line or *way* on the other side of the tee?" He quickly replied, "Of course it's going to be way, *way* on the other side of the tee." You know, sometimes we believe what we want to believe. I should have asked to look at the drawings for the course layout . . . oh, well. Thank God big leafy hedges grow quickly in Palm Springs.

7. What Have They Got Planned Next Door?

Choosing the lot or picking the best spot? Can you see the neighborhood completed in your mind's eye? Buyer mistake: not investigating all surrounding properties and their development plans. What will they/could they be building next store or behind? Will it block your now clear view? Don't forget to take into consideration what the traffic patterns will be upon completion.

 BYB Buyer's Blunder: Trying to Buy New Construction Realtor-Free

Make sure you have your own Realtor to represent you on the purchase of any new construction home or condo. The developer's or builder's sales agents are in the employ of the developer or builder so they are not going to have your best interests as their first priority. Their job is to sell those condos or as many of the new houses in the development as they can. They are not being employed to get *you*—the buyer—the best deal. These are not bad people, they are just doing their job: selling as many units as possible.

Once again, I hear so many novice buyers who are under the impression that they will be getting a better deal by going directly to the developer's agents. News flash: developers typically set aside the money they must pay as commission to a broker who brings a buyer to the development. So when you show up and try to buy directly from the developer, you're only saving the developer money and putting your own deal at risk. It's clearly to your advantage to have a Realtor with you from the get-go. It won't cost you any more money but can protect you *and* your money!

Condos and Co-ops

First, let's talk about what exactly a condo is. Basically, a condo is different from a house in that you actually have a shared ownership with other people. Most people believe you own one unit in a condominium building. Actually, you own only the walls of the condo and the air space in between. And sometimes you don't even own the walls, just the airspace. However, in addition, you own a share of all the common areas and elements of that building, such as the hallways and the laundry room, the garages, the swimming pool, and the lobby.

The Pros

■ **Affordability**—Condos are generally more affordable and lower in price than single-family homes. In most metropolitan cities especially, housing prices are so expensive that condos are the starter home option for many people. And after the severe market downturn, condo prices dropped even more than home prices. Thus condos are more affordable now than ever.

■ **The only game in some towns**—In New York City, condos and co-ops are pretty much the only game in town, unless of course you have the superbig bucks to buy an entire town house. And in metro Chicago, condos are one of the residential mainstays.

■ **Access to better neighborhoods**—Condos allow home-buyers to move into better neighborhoods in more desirable parts of town. Often they're in central city locations, near public transportation, good schools, stores, restaurants, nightlife, fitness centers, and job opportunities. Developers are able to offer condos even in the best of neighborhoods for a lower price because it costs less when you put more units in a building on one piece of land.

■ **Extra amenities**—Condos may offer lots of great amenities like pools, gyms, entertainment or conference centers, and tennis courts that you don't personally have to worry about keeping clean or maintaining. Sure, you have to write that condo association check every month, but you don't have to be cleaning out rain gutters in the spring or raking leaves in the fall.

■ **Safety**—Condo buildings have a certain safety factor. They usually have security gates and entry system intercoms. And of course there is safety in numbers. Having neighbors close by and across the hall is a big deterrent to crime, and a comfort as well, especially for single buyers.

■ **Ability to turn the key and walk away**—You often hear people say that they just want a home that is easy to maintain and manage. Condos provide that. For people who travel or spend long hours away from home, condos are ideal. Lock the door and go.

The Cons

■ **First to go and the last to come back**—When the housing market falls, condos tend to decrease in value faster than single-family homes and take longer to come back when the market begins to rise again. In the recent real estate dip, developers flooded the market with an oversupply of condos in growth cities like Miami, San Diego, and Las Vegas. The excess inventory coupled with the subprime mortgage crisis drove condos down in price much faster than their single-family-home counterparts. Condos are always in unlimited supply, whereas single-family homes have limited supplies. You can only build one house on a single lot, but you can have twenty condos on the same piece of property.

■ **Association dues**—With condos you share some common areas as well as the cost of maintaining those common areas. As part owner of the building, you will have to be responsible for a portion of the swimming pool repair or the new roof or the new tiling that goes into the lobby or even the elevator that has to be replaced down the line. This is all part of your monthly maintenance fees and later on possible unpredictable assessments that may come up this year, next year, or in the future.

■ **Common walls**—Keep the noise down, folks. If you can hear your neighbors yelling, they can probably hear you playing your favorite pop hits on your iPod docking station. That's the price of sharing common walls.

■ **Condo board rules**—You have to play by the rules. You are now part of a group of owners and have to adhere to the condo association's rules. I have a friend who was charged $500 by her association as security when she had to move furniture. The fee was supposed to cover any damage the building sustained when she moved a new couch into her unit. Totally unnecessary, but she had to adhere to her building association's rules.

■ **An apartment feeling**—Most condos don't have the private outdoor space that homes do. Yes, you might occasionally do some grilling on your balcony, but your neighbor in the balcony above you isn't going to like it.

Condo Shopping Tips

Because you are buying into a building of similar units, you need to know what yours has that the others don't and vice versa. Does it have or lack any distinct features that could affect its value? Here are some features, beyond the number of bedrooms and the square footage, that you should review to get a good idea of the actual value of your unit compared to the others. These are the additional items that will help you know whether you're getting the best unit in the building or the worst.

Condo Shopping Checklist

❑ General location in the building—convenience for getting in and out of the building, access to the building's amenities.

❑ Noise levels in that part of the building near the unit.

❑ Views.

❑ Finishes—such as cabinetry, countertops in the kitchen and bathroom, quality of flooring.

❑ How much natural light in the unit.

❑ Floor plan.

❑ Neighbors—good and bad.

❑ Number of parking spots—and proximity to your parking spot. How far will you have to lug the groceries?

 BYB Tip: Check Out the Parking!

If you drive a large vehicle such as an SUV or minivan, make sure it will fit into the assigned parking spaces for the unit you are previewing. Imagine spending all your money on your great new condo, and then having to go out and buy a new smaller car!

You're Not Just Buying a Condo, You're Buying a Building

When condo shopping, it's so important to understand that you are not just buying a condo unit, you are really buying a part of a building. And you want to make sure that it is a healthy building. I'm talking about financial health. If the financial profile seems shaky, or if additional assessments for big-ticket items like new elevators or windows or a large-scale lobby renovation are needed, no matter how great a deal you think you may be getting on the price, you'll still have to be kicking in extra money in the form of assessments to bear the cost of the building's ailing finances.

 BYB Tip: The $100,000 Condo Question

I am going to give you the one single question your Realtor can ask that will save you thousands of dollars, and possibly keep you from jumping on board a condo building that will become a money pit:

"Has there been any discussion of possible future improvements, changes, renovations, or maintenance or any financial difficulties that would result in an assessment or charges to be leveraged against all condo owners?"

Make sure to get the answer in writing. The reason this question is critical is that the condo association board must answer honestly or it could be held liable. All condo meetings must provide notes that can be subpoenaed, so any discussion of assessments, current or future, could be proven.

Condo New Construction: Empty Buildings = Empty Promises

Buying a new or preconstruction condo can have all the same pitfalls as the ones we just discussed with new and preconstruction single-family housing. Many condo buildings have remained unsold and partially empty for quite a long time. Though the discounted price tag may be delightfully tempting, buying into a building that only has 20 to 50 percent occupancy can be dangerous. Not only will it be difficult for you to get the developer to continue the upkeep of the building until all of the units are sold, but any new expenses and improvements on the building may have to be split amongst the only existing owners of the building. Making your maintenance or assessments much higher in the future.

Seven New/Preconstruction Condo Shopping Questions You Need to Ask

1. What percentage of the building is sold? Don't let them placate you by saying the building is 90 percent in escrow or under contract. Deals fall out of escrow at an alarmingly high percentage in today's market. You want to know how many have actually sold.
2. If you are looking at a building that is partially empty, who is paying to run the place? The fees aren't bad when there are a hundred owners, but when there are just fifteen owners in the building, those expenses are divided up among far fewer units.
3. Are there any assessments currently pending? Can you provide the financials?
4. Is there a currently elected condo association board made up solely of homeowners? Or is the developer still making all the financial decisions about the building without the individual condo owner's input?
5. Does the building currently have a reserve fund in case of emergency?
6. If any of the common areas or other units are still under construction, what is the completion date?
7. How many units are owner occupied? Many banks have specific regulations for lending to units in buildings that are populated by renters and not mostly owner occupied.

Co-ops

Cooperative apartments are especially popular in large metropolitan cities like New York City. Basically, when you buy a co-op, you buy shares in the corporation that owns the building in which your unit is located. You may have heard about how clubby co-ops can get, especially in a city like New York where housing is hard to come by. Some co-ops boards are notoriously elitist and will wield their power in choosing who they want to fill the building. Co-op rules can also be troublesome, such as requiring a gi-normous down payment—30 to 50 percent in cash.

 BYB Tip: Get a Haircut to Buy a Co-op?

Co-ops can be excellent investments, but they can throw a few people off because they operate a bit differently than condos. Now, I don't want to intimidate you, but don't be surprised if the co-op board actually asks you to stop buy for a meet and greet. Yep, they oftentimes want to interview you to see if you would be a good match for their building. So dress nicely, and be on good behavior.

Multiunit Properties

A multiunit property can be a fantastic option for someone who wants to be a little bit hands-on, who doesn't mind sharing a property or being the occasional landlord. Oh, and who doesn't want a home that pays part, if not all, of its own mortgage! Having that additional income can really help offset your monthly carrying costs.

Four Types of Income Properties I Recommend

1. Duplexes—Sold as one property with two separate residences

2. Triplexes—Sold as one property with three separate residences

3. House with a guesthouse

4. House with a separate apartment or rentable room

I love these properties. In fact, my first home in Los Angeles was a duplex. It was a wonderful 1920s up-and-down duplex with terrific details and charm to it. I lived in the downstairs apartment and rented

My first home purchase in Los Angeles was this duplex. The rent from the upstairs unit allowed me to own the building yet live there for free.

out the upstairs unit. The most amazing thing about this property was that I was able to live there almost mortgage free because the rent from the upper unit covered the expenses.

The Pros

1. You may be able to live for free. With rent coming in from the other unit or units, you can have a big chunk of your mortgage and carrying costs covered.

2. It's such a fantastic benefit to know that someone else is handing you money each month to pay off your home's mortgage month after month and year after year.

3. A duplex or triplex or home with a guesthouse may not be much more expensive than a single-family home. But you have that extra income bonus.

4. A fantastic advantage to purchasing a multiunit property is that when you are ready to move up or move on, you can hold on to this property and keep it as an investment. This will become the first step on your road to building a real estate portfolio that will provide you with income for life.

The Cons

1. You will have to learn very quickly how to be a landlord.

2. While having one or two rental units to manage is not a massive undertaking, you will still be responsible for keeping them rented and keeping your tenants happy.

3. Multiunits have at least twice as many things to repair and maintain—two or more kitchens, lots of bathrooms, two heating systems, two sets of plumbing, etc.

A 1920s Spanish fourplex that I currently own and rent out. It has an owner's unit in it that would enable a homebuyer to purchase this building, live in it, and have most of the building's mortgage payment covered by the rents.

4. You give up some privacy. You may have to share a backyard, driveway, hallway, laundry room, or garage with your new tenants.

As I write this book, I am currently renovating another wonderful multiunit property, a 1924 Spanish Revival fourplex. This one is so perfect for a homebuyer looking to live mortgage free. This fourplex has three beautiful units for rent, and one unit that can be earmarked as the owner's unit. And as it's an older building I get to do all my favorite fix-ups. There is something I find so fulfilling in bringing back the original charm and detail to an older home. In fact, one of the units had remained mostly untouched since the '20s. So it was actually less expensive to simply restore the original tile and hardware than to get all new.

Have Some Strangers Pay Off Your Mortgage

So, even as I list all the pros and cons, I think purchasing a home with income potential is a brilliant way to safeguard yourself in today's market. Yes, you do have to kick in some extra time to be a part-time

One of the living rooms of my Spanish fourplex. An added benefit to buying an older home or multiunit is restoring the original charm of the period.

landlord, and you will have to fix someone else's leaky faucet on your day off. But in the long run, it's an excellent way to buy a home, have a great place to live, and pay off your mortgage with the help of strangers!

What You Learned in This Chapter

♦ Consider the pros and cons of older/existing/fixer homes compared to new and preconstruction homes, as well as condos and co-ops, when shopping.

♦ There are four categories of older/existing/fixer homes: Mint Condition, the Cosmetic Fixer, the Downright Ugly house, and the Teardown.

♦ Fixer-uppers can mean money in your pocket and are a fantastic way to get into a house at a price you can afford.

♦ You need to estimate your fix-it costs before you make an offer on an existing house.

♦ Beware of the seven land mines when purchasing new construction.

♦ Take your checklist when you shop for a condo, and ask the right questions.

♦ When you buy a condo, you are actually buying a building.

♦ A multiunit property is a fantastic way to buy a home and have someone else pay your mortgage.

CHAPTER 7

Work with a Realtor or Go It Alone?

Don't try to buy a house without working with a Realtor. Okay, that's it. You don't have to read this chapter now. But if you don't believe me or think I'm pushing the whole work-with-a-Realtor thing, then you had better read on to understand why it's so important, and to your smart home-buying advantage.

When it comes to buying a house, you don't need to know it all. In fact, it's better that you don't. You have heard the expression: a little knowledge is a dangerous thing. Well, if a little bit of knowledge gives you the false impression that you don't need to be surrounded by professionals, then, yes, it is dangerous. It's so important to "know what you don't know." To be a successful homebuyer, you need to rely on the expertise, knowledge, and professionalism of the experts.

What a Realtor Can Do That You Can't

Realtors know the business inside and out. They have experience with each and every step of the home-buying and -selling process. They are the experts in a number of areas critical to the process, whether you're buying your first house, or your fifth. I always work with a Realtor. Always. Even if by some chance I have come across a property on my own or heard about one, the first call I make is to my Realtor to put his professionalism into action and to put the deal together. Here's what a Realtor's got that we don't:

- Access to every home that's on the market via the MLS (Multiple Listing Service) and all other sources, including ones that may not be listed publicly

- Inside track to the deals before they even hit the market

- The ability to combine your Dream House Checklist with your price range

- Knowledge of recent comps (comparables)—what similar properties have sold recently and for how much

- Knowledge of neighborhoods

- Ability to negotiate with the sellers on your behalf

- The inside scoop from the sellers' agents

- Expertise to negotiate and close the deal

- Experience to manage the legalities of foreclosures or other distressed properties

- Muscle to get a deal through the escrow or "under contract" period

- A litany of referrals for inspectors, mortgage brokers, and even tradesman for renovations

- Objective professional advice when you have your buyer's remorse meltdown

Keep in mind, too, that today's home purchase agreements can span ten pages or more, so your agent will need to handle lots of paperwork. That doesn't even include the federal- and state-mandated disclosures, and any documents required by local custom. One little, seemingly innocuous mistake or omission could cost you thousands.

Brokers, Realtors, and Agents

To be honest, it took me a long time to get these distinctions straight. It was not until I wrote my first book that I was able to figure them out. So let me explain them to you. In selecting a Realtor you'll need to know the difference between a broker, agent, and a Realtor. The difference varies from state to state, but in most places, you must be a licensed broker in order to list a property for sale. Brokers usually own the realty company and can hire agents and Realtors to work for and with them. Brokers are the "bosses" in the real estate business.

The difference between an agent and a Realtor is simple but important. An agent can only be called a Realtor if he or she belongs to the National Association of Realtors. By doing this, the agent signs a code of ethics and is bound by them. A big advantage of working with a Realtor is that if there is an issue between your Realtor and the other party's Realtor, not only can you take that agent's broker (boss) to task, but you can have disputes settled by the local realty board. Also, to qualify as a Realtor, an agent must participate in additional training and certification. You can work with any of them, but generally try to work with a licensed Realtor or broker.

How to Find the Perfect Realtor

There are *a lot* of Realtors out there today. Chances are you may already know one from within your own social circle. You can get referrals from neighbors, friends, and family members. But one word of caution is this: Don't pick someone so close to you that you can't have a serious "straight talk" business conversation. You need someone with whom you are not uncomfortable disagreeing. And keep in mind that this person will at some point become quite intimate with your entire financial picture.

You are going to be spending a lot of time with your Realtor, so his or her style had better be compatible with yours. Do you need someone easygoing or someone aggressive? Personally, I am a self-proclaimed overachiever and I like working with someone similar, as long as that agent has an easygoing personality and a great sense of humor. But you say, "I may not like him, but he is a real bulldog and will fight for a deal." You know what? If you don't like this Realtor, then chances are no one else will, either.

So choose the most qualified person for the job that you think you'll work well with. The ideal person for you is an experienced professional who knows your market, acts in an ethical manner, answers all of your questions and addresses your concerns, and most important, will listen to you and be your teammate throughout the entire process.

Look for Marketing Materials That Stand Out

I am always watching for a Realtor who markets himself or herself and the properties well. Pick up the local paper. Which Realtors advertise extensively? Who has great-looking ads and photos for their listings? Who seems to be doing an aggressive job of marketing their properties in the Sunday home section? Look at your mail. Is there one Realtor in particular that consistently sends eye-catching mailings? These are all signs of a Realtor who is hardworking and has marketing savvy.

Look for Someone Who Is Internet Savvy

As we discussed, a huge percentage of buyers will start their search on the Internet even before they contact a Realtor. Make sure your Realtor has a Web site and Internet presence. The Internet is also a great way to check your Realtor candidates' marketing skills and style.

Beware of getting referrals for agents through the Web. A Web site that refers you to certain agents is getting paid to make this recommendation. A better idea: Use a search engine to find the top real estate companies in your area and then spend time on their Web sites. Read profiles of individual agents at offices near you and look for testimonials from customers.

BYB Tip: Go Straight to the Top

Jim Gillespie suggests that if you are looking for a Realtor, go straight to the manager or broker of your local realty office. Tell him or her you want a Realtor with extensive experience in your neighborhood, someone who has been actively buying and selling homes for a long time. The manager will have a vested interest in your satisfaction and in keeping your business. He or she has an overview of all the Realtors' skills and will suggest the one best for you. Look around, too. You just might find a "wall of fame" close by that honors the office's top agents. Keep a lookout.

A Word for the New Guy

Just 20 percent of the agents do 80 percent of the business. But I'm a big believer in supporting the underdog, the new guy, the novice. Listen, we all started somewhere.

I remember walking into the office of my executive producer Lisa Gregorisch-Dempsey at *Extra* many years ago. I knew nothing about hosting and even less about producing. I was just finishing up my ten-year stint starring on CBS's *Young and the Restless*. Lisa asked me, "What kinds of things interest you, Corbett?" I told her all about my love of real estate, of fixing up and flipping homes, and that I had been doing it since I was twenty-one years old. She said, "Great—start tomorrow—you are going to host our real estate segments!" So, were it not for the wonderful people in my life who took a chance on me when I was green in acting and the new guy at hosting and then producing, I never would have accomplished my goals and lived my dreams.

That's why I also believe that, yes, a Realtor needs a few years of experience under his or her belt, but I am also willing to give a promising starter a shot, too. A neophyte's inexperience can be balanced by his or her drive, hunger, fresh approach, and enthusiasm. So even though I recommend someone with at least five years' experience in selling, don't overlook a hardworking fresh face.

Avoid the Part-Time Realtor

Avoid anyone who isn't serious about the real estate business as a career. You want someone who has helped people like you find and buy homes many times and who makes it a full-time job. Anyone who dabbles in real estate for supplemental income or as a part-time job is a no-no. This is too important of a business deal for you.

Work the Neighborhood

Another great way to get a pulse on potential real estate agents is to go to open houses and meet some who are actually in their work environment. Collect their business cards and jot notes on them. Are they polite and informative? Do they take an interest in your questions and appear knowledgeable about the neighborhood?

You can gather clues to help you make a wise choice of Realtors working in your area. It's also a good idea to track neighborhood signs. Pay attention to the listing signs in your neighborhood. Make note of when the For Sale sign goes up and when the Sold sign appears. The agent who sells listings the fastest might be working harder than other agents and will be working hard on your behalf to find the home you're seeking. Results speak volumes.

Questions to Ask a Real Estate Agent

As you begin to identify possible Realtor candidates, here are a few questions that you should ask to help narrow down the field.

- What percentage of your clients are buyers (vs. sellers)?

- In which neighborhoods do you primarily work?

- Will I be working with you directly or handed off to anyone else other than you? In other words, will you handle all aspects of my transaction or will you delegate some tasks to a sales associate or administrative assistant? A knowledgeable assistant can be invaluable, but you want to make sure you can connect with your agent regularly.

- Do you work full-time or part-time as a real estate agent?

- How many homes have you closed in my neighborhood?

- How many other buyers are you representing now? How many sellers? Hint: the busiest agents often are the most efficient.

- Is your license in good standing? You should check an agent's certification yourself with your state's Department of Real Estate. Many states provide this information online. For example, in California residents may check at www.dre.cahwnet.gov/licstats.htm.

- How many years of education and experience do you have? Experience and continuing education typically make for better agents.

- Are you also a broker and/or a Realtor or an agent? (I explained the differences earlier, and it's good to know which you are dealing with.)

- Can you provide me with the names and phone numbers of past clients who have agreed to be references? Insights from past customers can help you learn more about an agent and give you a greater comfort level.

How to Work with Your Realtor

One of the things you will always hear me preach about is integrity in business. I am believer that if you operate with integrity and treat other people with respect, they will treat you with respect in return. Once you've selected a Realtor and set him or her on the path of finding your dream home, show some loyalty. That person is working hard to find you a house. Don't string along several Realtors at the same time all searching the same MLS for you. Don't waste everyone's time as they all do double and triple work for you. Work with one.

On the other hand, if you are unhappy with your Realtor, tell him why, try to work it out, then switch if you feel you need to. But make sure you let him know.

A very good Realtor friend of mine, Brian, once worked with a client for six months, tirelessly showing this client, whom we'll call Clay, house after house. Clay ran Brian around town weekend after weekend looking at homes. One weekend Brian called Clay to set up some new showings, and Clay announced that he'd just placed an offer that morning using another agent, a friend of his. And of course it was one of the houses that Brian had been set to show him that very day. During all those months this sleazy fellow had run Brian around looking at properties, and in the end he handed the actual deal and the commission to a buddy.

I bumped into Clay a few weeks later. I told him that what he did was unethical and downright crappy. His response: "Hey, that's good business." My response: "No, that's bad business and even worse character." Ironically, I was later asked by a colleague for a character reference for this guy. As you can imagine, I was unable to give him a favorable recommendation.

Understanding Commissions

Let me make this easy for you to remember: Sellers pay the Realtor's sales commission, so as a buyer, you really needn't concern yourself with the logistics of paying commissions and figuring out how much you have to pay them. The commissions get deducted from the proceeds that the seller receives upon the sale.

 BYB Tip: Be Careful of a Dual Agent Situation

An agent is there to protect your interests in the transaction of buying a house. So it can get complicated if the house you want to buy happens to be one that is listed by the agent you are working with. This is a local thing with local rules but some states do not allow a Realtor to represent both buyer and seller. But know that some states do allow this if proper disclosure forms are filled out. If you find yourself in this situation, ask to be represented by your Realtor's office broker. This will keep things clean and create some distance between you and your seller so you can have more negotiating power.

According to REAL *Trends*, the average real estate commission is now 5.1 percent. And the rate is usually negotiable. If you ask around in your area, you'll find that most work for a commission in the same ballpark. But again, as a buyer you don't need to worry too much about this department. The burden is on the seller—not you.

What You Learned in This Chapter

♦ Never try to buy a house without the help of a professional.

♦ Avoid working with anyone who is not a full-time agent or Realtor. Avoid working with a friend who is a Realtor with whom you are not comfortable discussing your private financial details.

♦ A great way to find the right Realtor for you is to go straight to the top. Ask the manager of your local real estate office to suggest someone.

♦ Be careful not to get stuck in a dual agent situation, where your agent is representing both you and the seller.

CHAPTER 8

Three Steps to House Shopping

So you now have a good basic idea of what your ideal house could look like, and a list of must-haves and should-haves. You even have a realistic idea of how much you can actually afford. You have selected a Realtor and are ready to buy! Well, not quite yet. Let's put all this information to use first—and start shopping!

Shopping Reality Check

It's time to get down to business. And time to get real. You have to realize it's possible you have inflated expectations of what your money will buy. On the other hand, after all the downturns in today's market, you may be pleasantly surprised. You might find the house deal of the decade. Either way, you won't know whether you have found a deal or an overpriced dud unless you have worked the three steps to house shopping.

In my other books, I use analogies that compare home buying and selling to dating. For example, I explain that getting your house ready to sell is a lot like going out with someone for the first time: "You want to create curb appeal, because a pretty face will get them in the door!" When it comes to home shopping, the process is a lot like finding the perfect mate. We have all heard "you have to kiss a lot of frogs to find a prince." Well, the same holds true in the house-hunting world.

The Three Steps

No matter what you are shopping for, you won't know you have a great deal until you shop around and compare. It's getting out there and kicking the tires. You must become educated as to what is available, what homes really cost right now, and what your money will really buy.

The key to successful house shopping is to do it in three waves, or steps. You begin with the big picture and the easiest information to access, then you get out there and really walk the beat. Finally, once you have a very good idea of the value, pricing, and availability of your ideal home, you and your Realtor will start to examine the actual candidates. That's three steps.

1. Surfing the Internet

2. Attending open houses

3. Shopping seriously with your Realtor

BYB Tip: Don't Skip a Step

Don't try to buy the first house you see. Even if you think the house is absolutely perfect and it's everything you could want, shop around—if for no other reason than to reassure yourself that the house you found on day one really *is* the smart choice for you. If you don't continue to shop, you'll have nothing to compare it to and it will just lead to anxiety, self-doubt, second-guessing, and ultimately a major case of buyer's remorse later on.

House Shopping Step 1: The Internet

Let your fingers do the walking. Did you know that today 84 percent of all buyers begin their house shopping online? It's the best way to get familiar with the market, the houses, the prices, the neighborhoods, and the current inventory without leaving your home or office. The Internet is an invaluable tool for house hunting, much more than it was even three years ago.

You are not going to buy a house while online shopping, and you won't necessarily find the house of your dreams or the bargain of the year. But with every click of that mouse you become a more educated, smarter home shopper. And a smart buyer gets a better house and pays less.

Instant Access

Homebuyers now have access to real estate information that previously was only available to Realtors and industry professionals. According to Trulia.com's consumer expert, Tara-Nicholle Nelson, the Internet has become an essential part of any real estate transaction, from searching for properties to purchase to comparing similar properties to marketing properties you want to sell. It's so easy to get instant access to a property's current and up-to-date value and a good ballpark idea of prices in each neighborhood. But most important, you will get an invaluable education about how much or how little your money will buy.

How to Use the Internet to House Shop

The minute you finish this chapter, jump on your computer and start surfing. Seriously. You will see a healthy sampling of houses in your price range on the market at this very minute. The Internet is a window on the widest cross-section of properties available. Get in the habit of checking these realty Web sites every few days. You will see what is selling and what is sitting. Try going to www.Coldwell Banker.com, www.trulia.com, www.realtor.com, and the other sites listed in the Internet resource guide at the back of the book. Plug in your zip code. Put in the minimum and maximum price range and . . . bam.

You even have the ability to get a ballpark idea of any specific house's current value. Give it a try. Look up your boss's or brother-in-law's house, or how about that dilapidated house next to your daughter's nursery school? Go to www.zillow.com. Plug in the address. With a few keystrokes you now have a general, basic idea of what that house is worth.

Walk the Block with Google Maps

It's amazing to me, but not only can you find photos and video tours of homes online these days, you also can now actually "walk the block" and look at the neighborhood from the street level.

Powerful tools at www.google.com/maps now allow you to really "see" a whole neighborhood. You can also check out the condition of the surrounding properties. You are literally able to see the front yard of the house across the street. And you're able to look at other houses on the block for a street view. Any abandoned cars in the driveways? Could your dream home actually be next door to a cemetery or busy freeway? Click away and check it out.

Just Browsing, Please

Now, don't get too excited by what you see on the Web. No jumping ahead of the shopping process. Remember you are in step 1 of your house shopping juggernaut. This is simply the time to look around. Just like going into a car dealership for the first time to look at the new models as five salespeople rush toward you. "Just browsing."

If you see a house or condo you love, then print it out. Hold on to the printouts for reference later. You are going to want to compile all your printouts and brochures that you will gathering up in this step and in step 2. You will be handing them all over to your Realtor in house shopping step 3. You are not ready to buy yet!

But It Looked So Good on the Screen

A warning to the smart house shopper: you will discover, once you start clicking and scrolling, that many of the properties that look good on the screen may not look all that hot in person. It's kind of like that in the entertainment business, too. Believe me, on my show *Extra*, I have interviewed many top Hollywood celebrities. Some are even more beautiful and striking in person, but many times they are quite plain and ordinary up close. You wouldn't necessarily notice them if you passed them on the street.

The same is true for photos and videos of houses shown on the Web. A little retouching and wide-angle shots can go a long way. Just ask some good friends of mine, who regularly give me grief about the cover shot on my last book! Just so you know, I take no responsibility for any retouching . . . that was all done by the publisher's art department!

If a listing real estate agent is smart, you'll be seeing the very best of what that house has to offer online, and I can promise you that the dilapidated garage of the next-door neighbor's house has been cropped out of the shot.

 BYB Tip: Not Always the Latest and Greatest Info

Be aware also that you probably aren't going to find any amazing deals online. The kinds of hot properties and steals you want are often gone before they hit the public realty Web sites. Also, you may not find information on every home for sale in a particular neighborhood. So if you relied on the Internet alone, you'd miss out. Not only that, you may not be viewing the latest information. Many times Realtors don't update properties as sold because they still want to receive the calls in hopes of directing you to one of their other listings. Some sites don't upload new content as quickly as others and data could be a bit outdated.

The MLS

What is the MLS? The Multiple Listing Service—MLS—is a data bank that contains all the important information about properties that have come on the market. Prior to a few years ago, the information in the MLS was guarded and inaccessible to anyone other than Realtors and brokers. Well, the Internet has changed all that. Almost all of it is online now—all the information you need at your fingertips twenty-four hours a day. There can be a difference between what you'll find on the actual MLS and what's on sites like www.realtor.com or similar destinations. The MLS is a very up-to-date and accurate resource. At www.mls.com, you'll find the portal to local MLS listings, though some of the links will require you to register.

Unlocking the Secret Language of the Listings

The MLS and all other realty Web sites and listings seem to have language all their own. To the untrained eye, the properties described sound amazing. But the key is to unlock the real meanings. Here's a reality check translation guide:

- **Charming:** Small.

- **Cozy:** Even smaller.

- **Needs TLC:** Needs a remodel.

- **Partial view:** If you are standing on the roof, or you lean out the second-floor window.

- **Handyman's special:** That's a three- to four-hammer job. You'll be hunting down contractors for help with this one.

- **Up-and-coming neighborhood:** Paint your fence with antigraffiti spray.

- **As is:** There is something very wrong that the seller doesn't want to fix.

- **Diamond in the rough:** No jewel here—way too much work.

House Shopping Step 2: Open Houses— Look, Don't Touch!

This is the best part of house shopping. I love going to open houses. I will bring my car to a screeching halt when I see an Open House sign. I can spend an entire Sunday afternoon looking at homes on the market—even if I am not looking to buy.

It's fun because there is no pressure. You are "just looking." That's it! Just learning and seeing what kinds of things you like and don't like. You're also checking out what your dollar will really buy . . . in person.

Open houses are the next step after your Internet searches. You've gone from the two-dimensional into the three-dimensional realm where you get to feel and touch and experience the houses. You also get to explore and evaluate the neighborhoods up close and personal.

And even if you find a house that you fall in love with, again: no pressure. You aren't going to put an offer on it that minute. You will be looking at a half dozen other houses very soon with your Realtor and of course you can throw that one in the mix and see how it stacks up. So have fun. Enjoy the process. Every open house you see will better educate and prepare you.

 BYB Tip: Tell Your Realtor

Let your Realtor know you're doing an open house shopping spree! Make it clear to your Realtor that while he is looking on your behalf, you will be looking, too, and if you find something, you'll bring him in to write the offer and do the deal. This statement shows loyalty on your part and will inspire hard work on his.

Dos and Don'ts of Open House Shopping

1. **Eliminate the hard sell.** Walk in, shake the listing agent's hand, introduce yourself, and mention the name of your real estate agent immediately. Nine times out of ten this will eliminate those hard-sell pitches by the agent covering the open house. Odds are, the agent is going to ask you to "register," or sign in. To avoid unsolicited sales calls, you should provide your Realtor's contact information.

2. **Who is this person?** It's okay to ask if he or she is the listing agent. Usually the listing agent knows the most about the house. However, sometimes the listing agent is double-booked or too busy, so if it's another agent holding the house open for

the listing agent, that person may be more willing to tell you some of the inside scoop, such as the sellers' flexibility or a few of the problems of the house.

3. **Let the agent do the talking.** This is when the agent should try to impress you with all features of the home . . . newer roof, copper plumbing, etc., and give you the sales spiel. If the agent has nothing to say then either the house is a dog or the agent is not doing his or her job.

4. **Don't reveal too much about yourself.** Of course always be polite and cordial, but try not to reveal information about yourself or your situation or need to buy. Especially . . . *never* reveal the top price you are willing to pay. If you are indeed interested in this house and you end up making an offer down the line, you don't want any of that information to be used against you in negotiation. Hold your cards close to your chest.

5. **Keep your interest under wraps.** If this is the perfect house for you and you are itching to call your Realtor on the spot, don't do it. Keep a poker face, thank the agent for his time, and retreat out to the car. Drive a block away, then call your Realtor to tell him you have found your dream home!

   Yes, drive away. When I sell a house, I always want to know if the buyers stick around outside to discuss the house after they have viewed it. If they are in their car jumping up and down and on the phone, then I know I have "got 'em." I win and the buyer loses his leverage!

6. **Collect the flyers.** Take away the takeaways . . . the brochures or the printout information sheets on the houses you see, to keep track. Save them to show to your Realtor.

 BYB Buyer's Blunder: Buying Directly from the Listing Agent Thinking You'll Get a Better Price

You are at an open house; you love the place. And you think, wow, I'll bet if we get this listing agent to make our offer for us, we will save a bundle in commissions and price. Wrong! The seller's agent owes you nothing. This listing agent will not necessarily be loyal to your goals and wishes. The amount of money you will lose because

no one is negotiating solely on your behalf far outweighs any meager price break you think you would be getting.

Remember the commission is paid by the seller, and the selling
agent wants the house to sell for as much as possible. Also, negotiations don't stop once your offer has been accepted. Oh, no, they
have just begun, as you will see as you read on. And you're going
to need someone supporting and negotiating for you until the very
last day of closing.

The same holds true if you call the broker listed on an online
site for more information about a particular house—tell that listing
agent that you already have representation.

House Shopping Step 3:
Serious Shopping with Your Realtor

Okay, so let's look at what you have already accomplished. It's a lot:

- You have surfed up a tidal wave on the Internet.

- You've attended a few open houses—looking but not touching.

- You now have a realistic idea of what is out there on the market in your price range.

Nice job, good work. You have now transformed yourself into
an educated, knowledgeable, well-informed, realistic, and prepared

buyer. You are well ahead of the pack and poised to make a smart, sensible, and money-saving home choice. I can promise you, you have already saved yourself thousands of dollars by being able to spot a great deal when it is presented to you. You are now ... an empowered buyer.

The Buyer's Preparation Package

You have selected a Realtor you want to work with. You are ready to buy. You did your homework. Now is the time for you to get on the same page with him or her by sharing all your homework and research. You and your Realtor are about to become a team. As such, he or she now needs to have a pretty good idea of what you are looking for, and what your dream house and neighborhood should be.

Getting your Realtor up to speed with what you want is going to be relatively easy now. At this point you're this agent's dream client because you're prepared, which in turn makes it easier for him to find you the best house at the best price.

You have now four items that you're going to turn over to him. Think of these four items as all part of your Buyer's Preparation Package.

The Buyer's Preparation Package

1. **Your Dream House Checklist**—Since creating your original list, you've likely made a few changes to your must-haves and should-haves. You've had to adapt the list and make a few compromises based on what you discovered during shopping steps 1 and 2. Do a final update to your list and hand it over.
2. **Internet Printouts**—These are the printouts of all the properties that you liked or were drawn to for some reason while you were surfing and browsing the realty Web sites. Nothing is worse than when you try to describe your ideal house to the Realtor and turn to your significant other and say: "Honey, what was that house we saw online that was just perfect for us? I want one just like that! If I could only remember the address!"

3. **Flyers from Open Houses**—The same holds true for the open house flyers and brochures. With flyers in hand, you can discuss the pros and cons of the open houses you have already seen.
4. **Preapproval Letter for a Mortgage Commitment**—As we discussed in chapter 4, having that preapproval letter is your fast track to snagging the great deal. It makes you a stronger buyer and lets the seller know you mean business. It means you can get a mortgage, which in today's market is a fantastic trump card to be holding. Make sure you hand over a copy of it to your Realtor.

Your Realtor's Turn to Shine!

Now is when your Realtor gets to do his job; looking for properties is what he does. Finding the right one to match your must-haves and should-haves is his forte. By the time the Realtor has reviewed your Buyer's Preparation Package with you, he will be ready to begin his selection process of existing homes for sale. He will match your criteria to what is available and select properties to show you that hit as many of your requirements as possible.

What You Can Expect from Your Realtor Now

- Review your Buyer's Preparation Pack with you.
- Scour the MLS or other real estate listing sites in your area.
- Talk to other Realtors in his office and other franchise offices.
- Check out the current available bank repossessions, foreclosures, and short sales.
- Speak with potential sellers.
- Scope out the inside deals. A good Realtor has his ear to the ground. The great ones hear about properties even before a seller makes his first call to a listing agent. Furthermore, agents talk to each other constantly. Information is their currency, and

they trade it as it suits their goals. In highly competitive markets, Realtors have "in-house" listings that never even make it to the MLS. Agents will announce a hot listing to the other agents in their own home office, giving that entire home office a first shot at selling the property.

- Prescreen properties to make sure they are within your parameters.

- Prepare a list of approximately six to ten properties that he will escort you through.

- Take you house shopping.

How Many Houses Do You Need to See?

Here in step 3, how many houses will you look at before you buy?

According to Bill Riss of Coldwell Banker, Seattle/Portland, there's a rule of thumb that most experienced agents understand: a prepared buyer who has been shown twelve properties that fit his or her needs will quickly narrow those to three, one of which they're likely to purchase. But a buyer who asks to be shown more and more homes, without narrowing the field and moving toward a decision, is just not "ready."

You may not realize it but by this point in your house hunt, you will have looked at fifty to one hundred homes. What? Really? I didn't have time for that, you say. Not to worry, most of these have been from the comfort of your desk chair. And a good dozen of them have been viewed on a few leisurely Sunday afternoons of open house shopping. Now that you have completed steps 1 and 2, here in step 3, if you're truly ready and able to buy, when your Realtor starts showing you houses, it's possible that you may find the right one for you in that first batch.

Shopping Day One

A good real estate agent will review your Buyer's Preparation Package, compile all your must-haves and should-haves and even a few "wow, I wish I could haves," and arrange to show only those homes that fit your particular parameters. Some of the homes he puts on your shopping list will be ones he has already seen; others may be so new that he has not yet previewed them, either.

Most Realtors will work one of two ways. In this Internet age, he or she may compile eight to ten properties that are a match for you and then send them to you online. This gives you a chance to "prescreen" and review them. By now you have already gained some expertise looking at properties online, so this prescreening will be very helpful. You'll be looking through the MLS listings and/or Web site pages he sends you to see if there are any that you want to immediately nix from the list.

Other Realtors may just set an appointment time, pick you up, hand you a short stack of printouts, and take you out straight away.

Your first day out and about, you might expect to see seven or eight houses. You will love some and hate some, but by the end of the day, both you and your Realtor may already have a few favorite candidates out of the bunch.

How to Shop—Keeping Track

You may think you'll be able to remember the location and details of every house that has caught your eye. But in the heat of the hunt, you won't. That's why you are going to ask the Realtor ahead of time to provide you with a copy of all the information sheets for each of the houses you are going to preview. I warn you that after a while, usually around the fourth or fifth house, they are all going to become a blur of bedrooms, countertops, and crown molding. You're going to forget which one had the enclosed porch and the two and a half baths, which one had the small center hallway but the skylight in the kitchen, and which one had the big master closet but not a separate laundry room.

It's imperative that you keep track of each prospective house. You want to remember the features and amenities of each. Make notes on the printouts from the Realtor. Jot down questions, a special feature that you particularly loved, or even things about the house that may be wrong that you will want to investigate further if you decide to come back to that particular one for a second showing.

Your Overall Rating

Just as with most things in life, the whole is more than the sum of its parts. The same is true with a home. We have talked about many individual components, pros and cons, and house shopping tips on each kind of property. As you know by now, I am a big proponent of analyzing a huge purchase like this as a business decision. Be practical and smart.... However:

Now is the time to let your instincts join the party. You are going to create an "overall rating" for each house on a scale of 1 to 10. The overall rating is a chance to join together all the parts of the whole. Combine the crucial must-haves, wishful should-haves, price, and practicality along with your *feelings* about how much you actually *like* this house. This is your chance to let your emotions reign. But only for a moment!

How does this house feel? And how does it make you feel?

Now combine that ethereal instinctual vibe with all the practical pluses and minuses of the house. The result is your overall rating. You want to determine this overall rating immediately after leaving the house so that it's fresh in your mind. You'll refer back to this rating right before you make an offer, or especially if you need a tiebreaker for your final two or three choices.

Take a Picture, Why Don't You

Now that almost everyone has become tech savvy these days, an absolute must-have is a digital camera or a phone with a built-in camera. Every time you look at a house make sure you take a snapshot of the exterior. Grab a few shots of some of the rooms as well, especially the kitchen. Later, download the photo and label it with the address of the house. Begin each series of photos with a close-up of the house number to identify where each group of home photos starts and ends.

Look Beyond the Window Dressing

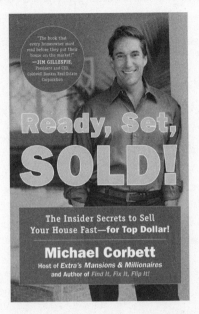

Don't be fooled by "RSS" sellers! I hate to admit it, but I personally may be responsible for you overpaying for your house. I can promise you if the seller of the home you're previewing has read my last book, *Ready, Set, Sold! The Insider Secrets to Sell Your House Fast—for Top Dollar!* you're in trouble! But not to worry, the key to counteract that is: don't buy emotionally, buy intellectually. If you can do that, you will save yourself thousands of dollars and avoid overpaying for your home no matter how enticing the sellers have made it.

Again, I am a homebuyer's worst nightmare because I have been teaching home sellers for years how to dress up their homes to pull at buyers' heartstrings. I have taught sellers to stage their homes, to create inviting vignettes, and to really snag a buyer emotionally by seducing his senses via sights, sounds, and even smells.

Here are some telltale signs of a *Ready, Set, Sold!* house:

- You walk into the home and hear softly playing music.
- You find perfectly clean, uncluttered, light-filled rooms.

- All personal items like trophies, photos, religious and political items, and little Frankie's kindergarten drawings have been sent to storage.

- Crisp, fresh white sheets make the beds reminiscent of a five-star hotel.

- An orchid sits on the bedroom nightstand.

- Pots of freshly planted colorful flowers sit by the front door.

- Maybe even the slight scent of fresh-squeezed lemons greets you in the sparkling clean kitchen. . . .

Be forewarned: You are about to deal with a very smart seller! And expect to be in competition with other buyers for that house. But don't be fooled; keep your emotions out of it and look beyond the window dressing.

 BYB Tip: The Hardest Ones to See Are the Best Deals

Especially in today's new market you need to be persistent. The hardest houses to get to see are usually the best buys. This is especially true with older homes, fixers, and distressed properties—foreclosures, short sales, etc. I am always delighted to hear that a seller or, better yet, the renter of the house has been making it difficult for Realtors and their clients to get in. That means that you are going to get a deal. Most buyers don't have the tenacity. They also don't get the deals.

The Market Temperature Affects Your Shopping Price Range

The temperature of the market will actually affect how you shop and the prices of the houses you should look at. Knowing how to tweak your shopping price range based on the direction of the market gives you more opportunity to hit your target price.

BYB Tip: Shop Higher in Today's New Market

—Barbara Corcoran, bestselling author and real estate expert

In a downward-moving (buyer's) market, always shop 10 percent higher than you really want to spend. Start at the top of your price range.

If you feel you can afford a home that is $400,000, then look at homes priced at $440,000. The reasoning is that in a cold buyer's market you will probably pay slightly under the asking price. There may be room to negotiate down to bring it into your price range, so shop approximately 10 percent higher than you are planning to pay.

Hot Market: Start at the Bottom

The reverse is true in a hot market. Start at the bottom of your range and work your way up. Oftentimes when the market is on fire and the sellers have the upper hand, you may have to pay more than the house is actually listed for. So be aware that if you can afford $400,000 in a hot market, you may have to look at properties priced 10 percent less at $360,000.

What You Learned in This Chapter

♦ You need to shop around—kick a lot of tires before you decide on a house.

♦ There are three steps to house shopping: (1) surfing the Internet; (2) attending open houses; and (3) shopping seriously with your Realtor.

♦ Don't skip a step. You will doubt yourself later.

♦ Get educated about what's out there, and what it really costs, by Internet and open house shopping.

♦ Not everything on the Internet is accurate and up-to-date.

♦ Don't buy the first house you see.

- ◆ Keep track of all the houses you loved while shopping in the first two steps.

- ◆ Avoid buying from the listing agent.

- ◆ Create a Buyer's Preparation Package so your Realtor can find you the perfect house.

- ◆ In step 3 you and your Realtor become a team as he or she utilizes all of his or her resources to find you the dream house.

- ◆ Educated buyers who have completed steps 1 and 2 will find at least one house they love within the first ten houses their Realtor presents.

CHAPTER 9

Foreclosures and Short Sales . . . Oh, My!

We've all heard it blasted across the late-night TV screens, on the covers of books about real estate deals, and of course in the break room at work where someone always has a friend of a friend of a friend who bought a foreclosure for next to nothing.

You think, well, this is fantastic, I am going to run out and find a foreclosure or a short sale and buy it for half price right now! That would be an amazing deal, right? Okay, duh . . . of course it would be an amazing deal if you snagged a house worth $600,000 and only paid $299,000.

Now it's time for a reality check. Which brings me to the next new rule.

So often homebuyers think they should focus all their shopping attention on so-called distressed properties, or what I call stressed-out properties—a term I'll use loosely to describe any property in foreclosure, short sale, or one that has gone back to the bank and is potentially up for auction. All of us have heard anecdotally that these types of houses are good deals. The irony is that most homebuyers probably cannot begin to define a foreclosure or a short sale and don't have any idea about the pros and cons of buying either one. However, because foreclosures and bank-owned properties are so abundant these days, they should be considered and we will talk about them in this chapter.

> ### New Rule: Just Because It's a Distressed Property Doesn't Mean It's a Good Deal
>
> *—Alexis McGee, founder and CEO of Foreclosures.com*
>
> Just because a house has been taken back by a lender or the government doesn't mean it's a winning deal for you. Don't assume that every house in foreclosure is automatically a steal. Remember, if it were a fantastic home and an amazing property, the original owner might have been able to sell it to get out of foreclosure. There is a reason it didn't sell. And even if it's currently priced well and it seems like a good deal, there are plenty of hoops you have to jump through and roadblocks you will have to overcome.

Good foreclosure and short sale buys are available, but you need to do your homework, understand exactly what you are getting into, be patient, and learn the foreclosure and short sale process before proceeding.

> **BYB Tip: Don't Expect to Buy Properties at Fifty Cents on the Dollar in Today's New Market**
>
> Rob Friedman, chairman of the Real Estate Disposition Corporation, explains that no one is going to sell you a property for half of what it's actually worth. That just doesn't make sense. What seller, or bank, no matter how strapped, crazy, or "motivated," is going to sell a property that is really worth $300,000 for $150,000? The public has become far too savvy. All any distressed owner or bank foreclosure department has to do is pick up a phone or go on a Web site to discover an appropriate value for the home.

Rob Friedman, one of the most successful real estate auction entrepreneurs, says that fifty cents on the dollar is all a bunch of hype. He auctions off REO, or real estate owned, properties for banks—sometimes up to two hundred a day. He knows that banks will not sell for fifty cents on the dollar. Even at the bottom of the market, the reality is that most auctioned properties sell for market value or only 15 to 20 percent below current market value *at most*.

Despite what you hear, banks do not want to give away any property, no matter how sharply it's dropped in value. Banks need to recoup whatever equity they can from them. Yes, they will discount them when the market is foreclosure-heavy, but as I just stated, the actual average discount is only 15 to 20 percent—not fifty cents on the dollar!

And here's the bigger hitch: 15 to 20 percent discounted off of what? Last year's value? The value of the latest comp sold? What the house was purchased for? See . . . buying a distressed property can be a tricky game of determining price versus the actual value of the property.

Don't Focus Only on Foreclosures and Short Sales

You don't need to pursue distressed properties exclusively to get a deal. Let me explain it this way. On the same block in Scottsdale, Arizona, are three identical houses. One of them is in foreclosure and on the market for $330,000. Another is a short sale and also accepting offers at $330,000. The third house is owned by a nice elderly couple who needs to move back east. At what price do you think they will have to list their house to get it sold? That's right, $330,000. Why would you overlook their house—a much easier transaction to close—just because you mistakenly think that the best deals are only foreclosures and short sales?

First, however, we have to distinguish between a foreclosure and a short sale. These terms get thrown around a lot, but many people are confused by what they mean exactly. It's important to know the difference because each comes with its own set of rules and challenges.

What Is a Foreclosure?

When a homeowner can't meet his payments, or refuses to make payments for whatever reason, the lender takes the property back. The bank or lender will declare the borrower in default and provide a demand letter specifying a final date by which the borrower must become current. To become current the homeowner would have to catch up with his delinquent payments and be current with his monthly payments. During this process and until the lender has completed the foreclosure process and obtained title to the property, the property is said to be in "preforeclosure" and remains under the control of the borrower (current "owner"). Oftentimes these properties will be listed on the market for sale as the borrower attempts to sell off the house to avoid the financial and credit impact of a foreclosure action.

Once a property has hit the foreclosure stage, approval of a sale may involve the lender. This is often because the price at which the owner is selling is lower than what he owes. In essence, it becomes a preforeclosure short sale. In addition, once the foreclosure is completed many states provide the borrower with what is known as a period of redemption. During this time the owner, or "seller," still has an irrevocable right to get back up to speed and pay off the default, including all foreclosure costs, back interest, penalties, and missed principal payments. He then regains control of the property.

See, I warned you it was a bit complicated.

Each state has different laws. HUD.gov, RealtyTrac.com, Property Shark.com, and ForeclosureS.com are among several sites offering summaries of the laws state by state, as well as information about how long the process can take and what rights the owner in default may have. Some procedures involve the courts while others do not. Once the property passes through certain phases, it's eventually ready to be sold at auction to the highest bidder, or put on the market and listed as a "Bank Owned."

BYB Tip: But I Thought You Said You Were the Owner

You may not always know if a homeowner is facing foreclosure and trying to make a quick sale happen before the bank takes possession. In order to avoid the negative stigma for the homeowner, it's possible that no reference will be made in advertisements regarding an impending foreclosure. This is yet another reason why I encourage you to work with a Realtor who will ask the appropriate questions and even conduct a search on the property through a title company or attorney to determine its actual status. It's a huge waste of your time and money to enter into a contract with the current homeowner only to be notified that even though you are in escrow, the seller can no longer sell it to you. You would have to go back to square one and try to buy it from its new owner—the bank.

What Is a Short Sale?

Anytime you buy a short sale, what you're doing is asking to buy a property for less than what the homeowners owe on the loan. The big caveat to short sales: The current owners must get the bank or mortgage holder to agree to this type of markdown sale. Not all lenders accept short sales or discounted payoffs, especially if they feel they can recover more of the principal by foreclosing on the house. And not all sellers, or all properties, qualify for short sales. Generally, the borrower must have a legitimate "hardship" such as a loss of income due to unemployment or medical situation in order to be considered.

Also, all too often the lender won't accept an offer from you until you've completed a full short sale package that entails providing all of your financial information and a fully signed contract with the seller. Your Realtor will be able to assess the likelihood of that short sale being approved at the beginning of the process.

Short Sales Are a Waiting Game

The seller may tell you that he has requested approval from the bank to let him sell his home in a short sale, but that literally could take months to get finalized. Clearly the lenders are understaffed and over-whelmed by the tremendous number of files being processed. I have seen too many homebuyers hung out to dry for months waiting to get a short sale approval, only to be disappointed and forced to being at square one again in their house shopping.

The Short Sale 101

Here's an example of how the short sale works mathematically: Let's say Harry the homeowner wants to sell his house. It's only worth $250,000 in today's market. But Harry still owes $325,000 on his mortgage. He needs the bank to agree to let him sell the house for only $250,000 and then "short" the bank $75,000. As you can imagine, the bank will not be happy about agreeing to take $75,000 less for Harry's mortgage payoff. Thus, the bank may not choose to respond quickly or to cooperate at all.

Although most short sales can take months, there's one exception to this trend. Lenders participating in the voluntary federal Home Affordable Foreclosure Alternatives (HAFA) Program are now obligated to respond to offers on "approved" homes within ten days of the offer submission. However, this program applies only to certain mortgages originated prior to January 1, 2009, on a borrower's principal residence.

BYB Tip: Short Sale Approved?

Look for short sale properties that have already been "short sale approved." That means the bank has agreed in advance to "sell short" and let the homeowner try to sell the house for less than he owes. A word of caution here: just because the bank has agreed to a short sale, that does not mean it will agree to any specific price ahead of time, and it can still take months to give a potential new homeowner a positive or negative response.

Generally speaking, short sales can take an excruciatingly long time to close even once an offer has been accepted. I once heard of a short sale that took place in February and generated lots of bids, but it still hadn't closed by June of the same year. If you're the one with the winning bid and you can't get the house to close so you can move in, it can be an arduous and frustrating process to endure—much more so than buying a home that doesn't fall in the distressed category.

 BYB Tip: Go for the Small Ones—They Move Faster

Michael Lario, Esq., a very prominent and sought-after real estate lawyer in Haddonfield, New Jersey, recommends looking for short sale properties that are held by the smaller banks. Generally, the smaller or local banks are able to move a property through the short sale process much more quickly than the big national behemoth banks. What's more, they are often easier to deal with and can get you responses and answers much more efficiently than the giants.

More Stressed-Out Options

Government repossessions—Banks and private lenders are not the only mortgage holders. The government also owns lots of homes. You can check out HUD-owned homes up for bid in your area by going to www.hud.gov. There you'll also find all the information you need to buy a HUD home. Note, if you are looking for a deal on a 6,000 square foot mansion, however, you won't find it, because these government-guaranteed loan programs are designed to assist low- and moderate-income homebuyers.

All properties available for purchase by the public are offered for sale at Internet listing sites maintained by management companies under contract to HUD. You would want your real estate agent, if he or she is registered with HUD, to submit an offer and contract to purchase on your behalf.

VA properties—The Veterans Administration also has a listing of homes from its loan program. Once the VA has foreclosed, it can sell a property to anyone—regardless of a buyer's military status. You can be a veteran or nonveteran and buy a VA house. How do you find and negotiate these deals? Have your agent contact the local real estate agent who represents the VA's property management program vendor, which generally places the properties for sale in the local MLS. For leads, you can try the Department of Veterans Affairs at www.homeloans.va.gov.

Fannie Mae– and Freddie Mac–owned homes—Fannie Mae and Freddie Mac are household names, even though you may not know what these organizations do. They are corporations chartered by the government, and they are the chief secondary lenders in America, underwriting most of the conventional mortgages. On average, Fannie Mae and Freddie Mac properties tend to offer a wider range of pricing and these homes likely have been better maintained than those taken back by HUD and the VA, so you may be able to find a gem here. And once again, if you're interested in one of these properties, have your real estate agent be the one who puts together the sale. For an online listing and more specific information about Fannie Mae homes, go to www.homepath.com; for Freddie Mac, go to www.homesteps.com.

Wow, That's Really a Deal . . . Or Is It?

A few months ago, I attended an open house for a property that was a short sale. When I asked the Realtor about the price, she said, "It's really worth $1.2 million but we're only asking for $850,000 today." She added that if the bank chose to hold on to the property it would then be worth $1.2 million. But since the bank wanted to get the house off its hands ASAP, it was "deeply discounting" the price to move the house fast.

Here's my problem with this Realtor's approach. You can't price a house based on past or future value. It's like the stock market. At any given moment, a stock is only worth what it can sell for *right then*. While a certain stock—or house—might be worth more, or less, in the future, no one can predict that future price. So in today's reality, price is based on today's sales power. So her "discounted" price sales pitch was . . . bull. A house is only worth what someone will actually pay for it at the time it's up for sale.

Thus, if the Realtor can only sell that house today for $850,000, then you know what it's worth? $850,000!

The Six Roadblocks

The bottom line: when a property is in trouble or in distress, it's critical to be far more cautious than when purchasing a traditional sale property. In addition to the stumbling blocks I discuss above in determining what a distressed property is really worth, there are many unknowns and six major roadblocks.

1. **More complicated**—Buying distressed properties is not as easy as one-two-three. And is certainly not for the inexperienced homebuyer, without the guidance of a Realtor with expertise in these types of properties. Foreclosures can entail complicated transactions, during which you have to stay on top of not only your legal obligations but also those of the homeowner—who may have more rights than you realize. And in certain states, as discussed above, even homeowners in dire straits have the legal ability to reclaim the property if they are able to prepay their debts.

2. **Cash only**—What makes foreclosures in particular such a challenge for first-time buyers is that such sales are often for cash only—a difficult or almost impossible hurdle for beginners. An additional challenge is competition with investors who typically have plenty of cash at hand. All too often the lender will accept a cash offer over a financed offer even if the financed offer is for a higher amount.

3. **Not always the lowest price**—Distressed properties also may not necessarily carry rock-bottom prices, even if they are selling way below what the previous owners bought them for.

4. **Not always a clear title**—Although it's very rare, it is possible that you won't get title insurance or other guarantees as to the state and condition of the house, and all the liens and loans that are held against it. You may think you would be buying the house free and clear. But imagine closing on a property only to find out, after the fact, that there is also an existing second or third mortgage or lien against it that needs

to be paid off! You would then be responsible to pay it off. A foreclosure property that is purchased without a clear title can be a clear nightmare.

Historically, most closings are completed with a title insurance policy in place and rarely are there situations where the buyer of the home has had an issue. But to be on the safe side, make sure you get a clear title report; if you can't, then walk away. Chapter 15 explains more on the clear title.

5. **Last-minute offers**—There is a chance that even if your offer is verbally accepted, someone can come in with a higher bid at any time until you have a fully completed contract in hand; and this may end up being several weeks after you thought you bought the home.

6. **"As is"**—Most distressed property deals are "as is." Which means it can wind up costing you way more than you bargained for if the house has hidden problems, and if it requires a considerable amount of money and work to bring it back to life. Inquire about disclosures and inspections. You are on your own if you can't get the lender who's selling the property to fess up to any problems with the house or to make any repairs, and more often than not the lender has limited knowledge of the property. Why? Because, chances are, the lender has never even stepped foot on the premises.

Never Go It Alone—Work with the Pros

Listen, if you come across a great foreclosure deal or a wonderful steal of a short sale, I am fine with that. And of course you can choose to scour the distressed property Web sites. And while the overall process of home buying is the same, as I have said above, there are many other hoops to jump through than those you'll encounter with a nondistressed home. The laws change monthly and the requirements and processes for sales shift as quickly as the moon shifts position.

You must work with a knowledgeable and experienced real estate agent and/or attorney on this. You need that extra expertise to help guide you through this complicated process and achieve three important goals:

1. Determine what the house is really worth.

2. Know exactly what you're buying for the price.

3. Abide by the laws in your state and local area so you don't miss out on something critical that makes your entire deal unexpectedly go bust at a later date.

 BYB Tip: Do Your Web Site Due Diligence

As with any industry, there are some dubious sites and services out there trying to cash in on the foreclosure and short sale market right now, so it pays to be sure you're using a reliable source. Before you sign up at Web sites that list foreclosures and short sales, check their "free" trial periods. Some of these sites provide a teaser level of information but require a paid subscription to receive the type of information desired by any serious buyer.

Not Even Easy for the Pros

Jim Gillespie himself—who has access to the best agents around—had his own challenges when trying to buy a short sale property for his kids. He recalled, "The process was one of the most challenging I've ever faced. It took over four months to get to the finish line, only for us to learn that there was a second mortgage on the property. Being in the business, I knew the process would be difficult and we were not under time constraints to buy. But still, when we got to the end and thought it was over, to find out we still had more hurdles to jump was disappointing. Patience was definitely a virtue and we eventually did get through it."

Beware Distressed Property Bait-and-Switch Pricing

I'll give you one more example taken from my own experience. A really trendy and hip condo building was constructed right in a busy, fun section of West Hollywood, California. From the outside it looked great and it was in a terrific location—within walking distance to stores, restaurants, and nightlife. Upon closer inspection, what looked flashy from the outside turned out to be cheap construction on the inside. The developer originally priced the units at a staggering $1 million. They were worth half that.

Needless to say, not a single unit sold, and the developer defaulted on the entire building. All the units went to auction. The auction was advertised everywhere and it created quite a buzz with the claim "Starting bids as low as $295,000!" So I went online, pulled up all the information, and found that the small print of the auction instruction sheet read, "Auction USA Associates not obligated to sell condo at the advertised price. A reserve [or bottom line] that *will not be disclosed* is the minimum amount to be accepted" (emphasis mine). That starting bid of $295,000 was a great marketing ploy, especially since the owners had no intention of selling at that price. Not a great deal for anyone trying to buy one of these "gems" for what the market would bear.

The Distressed Property Neighborhood

Last, here's something else to keep in mind when buying a distressed property: how has this house—and potentially others in the neighborhood—affected the overall feeling and value of the area? Distressed properties are often found clustered in less than desirable neighborhoods or areas of a city. In that case, the neighborhood itself may be in disrepair as more and more owners abandon their houses. Will you be stuck in a declining neighborhood that can take years to recover? It's important to know what is happening with foreclosures and delinquencies in the surrounding area. I often say, you are not just buying a home—you are buying a neighborhood.

What You Learned in This Chapter

♦ Just because it's a foreclosure or a short sale doesn't mean it's a good deal.

♦ Don't expect to buy a house at fifty cents on the dollar.

♦ You don't need to pursue distressed properties exclusively to get a great deal in today's market.

♦ Foreclosures present a unique set of roadblocks and hurdles to overcome.

♦ Short sales can take months to get approved. Don't expect to move in anytime soon.

♦ Don't try to buy a foreclosure or a short sale on your own; there are too many unknowns. You need to work with a Realtor who represents you and understands the state laws and regulations regarding these properties.

PART FOUR

Buying

CHAPTER 10

How Much Is This House Really Worth?

After working through the three steps to house shopping, you have narrowed down your choices and found one you love, or at least one that hits most of your must-haves and hopefully a couple of your should-haves, too.

You are very excited. You call your brother Peter in Pennsylvania to tell him about it. You e-mail photos to your best friends, Cheryl and Roxy. You may even drive a few friends past the house that same night to see it. But now what? Amid the mix of excitement and a bit of anxiety, what do you do next? Do you whip out the checkbook and start writing? Here's my advice: CALM DOWN! The key to buying smart and paying less in today's market is to put your business hat on first. You may think you are ready to write the offer. But, hold on . . . you don't have enough information about this house or this seller yet. You don't even know how much this house is really worth!

Go Back and Really Look

Keep in mind that at this point you have only walked through your new potential dream house maybe twice. And then of course the couple times you have driven by with your aunt Marge and your mother-in-law.

Interestingly, your sex may determine how many times you will have previewed the house before you know it's the one you want. According to a Coldwell Banker survey, women buyers are likely to make up their minds faster than men. Almost 70 percent of women surveyed decided the day they walked into the house that it was right for them, while 32 percent of men needed two or more visits. Thus, it will likely take multiple trips to the home before both members of a couple decide it is "the one." So if a spouse needs more time, be patient and try not to pressure him or her.

And did I say one more visit? Yep, it's time to go back there and really give it a proper examination. Whether it's an older home or a new one, bring along your Dream House Checklist and your Fix-It Hit List. They are great resources and references for you to keep track of pros and cons, problems and amenities. But most important, you and your Realtor are going to need to start asking some questions.

The Inside Scoop—What's Not in the Listing

Yes, it's time to do some digging, investigating, and information gathering. It's time for you and your Realtor to find out everything you can before you make an offer. There is no need to develop psychic abilities. Just become a home-buying sleuth. You'll want to know all there is to know about that property.

If "information is power," this will put that power on your side of the bargaining table. Not only will all this help you negotiate a great deal but you will use this information to make your offer the best it can be. Not to mention you'll unearth problems that could cost you big time once you become the owner.

What You Need to Know

- Who is the seller—are they motivated?

- The house's market history.

- Ten questions home sellers don't want you to ask.

- The neighborhood scoop.

Who Is the Seller—Are They Motivated?

Who actually owns this house? That's the first question. Eight times out of ten it is going to be the individual or couple currently residing in the house. In some cases, it could be owned by a family member who is selling it off for a deceased loved one. And of course it's possible that the house is owned by a bank or lender. Well, no matter who owns it, clearly someone wants to sell it. You and your Realtor now need to find out just how motivated that person or persons are.

People sell houses for a wide variety of reasons. They may want to move up. Their family may be getting larger or smaller, or they may be having unforeseen personal or financial problems. Because of a situation beyond their control, the seller may need cash now. And in today's market many homeowners are selling to avoid foreclosure.

What Makes a Motivated Seller

- Divorce

- Death in the family

- Job loss

- Job relocation

- Facing foreclosure

- Advanced age or illness

- The purchase of another house

- Sellers are upside down in their mortgage and owe more than it's worth

- If the bank owns the house, it may be carrying a huge portfolio of homes that it needs to sell off ASAP

These conditions often make sellers very flexible and/or desperate, or—as we say in the business—"motivated." As heart-wrenching as they can be, these life-stage, personal, financial, or event-driven factors make a seller highly motivated and give you leverage and power when you make the offer.

Find Out the House's Market History

The complete sales history of the property will also help you and your Realtor customize your offer. You'll want to know how long the house has been on the market and what other offers, if any, have been presented. That is invaluable information to have. Also, if there have been other offers that have been rejected, finding out what didn't work is also indispensable info.

If the property has only just been listed and put on the market, the seller will likely still be hopeful of receiving a full-price offer. If it's been languishing on the market for months, he may be getting a bit desperate. If it has just fallen out of escrow, meaning the house was under contract for sale but for some reason the deal didn't come together, he may now be into a deal on another house already and really prepared to deal.

Market History Questions Your Realtor Needs to Ask

- How long has the property been on the market?

- How many offers have been made?

- Have any been turned down? Why?

- Were any previous offers accepted?

- Has the property fallen out of escrow?

Ten Questions Home Sellers Don't Want You to Ask

Below are the ten questions home sellers don't want you to ask. You probably won't get to ask them yourself, so your Realtor will have to do the sleuthing. In fact, if the seller's real estate agent is any good, she'll make sure that you never come face-to-face with the seller.

Agents almost always have their sellers leave the property during showings so that they won't hover over prospective buyers, but also so they don't reveal information that would help the buyer negotiate a better price.

There is a lot of information that is not on the MLS or in the listing. Yes, your Realtor can pull up all kinds of information about the house, the owner, the taxes, the current mortgage, etc. But there are some things that you just need to ask. Every property has some little quirks that the seller hopes you don't discover. Some are minor. Others could cost you big bucks down the line. In a perfect world, owners would fess up and tell all when they fill out the property condition disclosure statements that most states require.

I am a huge proponent of disclosing everything and being completely honest when selling a house. Unfortunately, not all sellers operate under these same standards.

Ten Questions Home Sellers Don't Want You to Ask

1. **Why are you selling?** People have lots of reasons for selling. What you want to know is, how anxious are they to sell? This is a great question to ask simply because it's good to hear it directly from the sellers. Or if that's not possible, the "filtered" answer from their agent will have to do. As we just discussed, this gives you an insight to the sellers' flexibility.

2. **How much do you owe on this house?** This is a big one. If the house has gone down in value since they purchased it, which is very often the case in today's market, you need to know how much the sellers owe, to know the minimum amount they must sell it for. This will give you a good idea of how much or how little wiggle room the seller has to negotiate. He may be at his breakeven mark right now and cannot drop the price any lower without getting approval from the bank. Most sellers also have a fixed number in their head of how much they would need to walk away without owing any money. You most likely won't be able to offer less than that number.

   If they don't owe a lot on the house and have some equity

in it, you are in luck. They may have more flexibility to come down in price, giving you more negotiating room.

3. **What did you pay and how long have you owned the house?** People love to brag about what a good investment they've made or complain about how much value their home has lost in the past few years. If their home has gone up in value, they're excited about it. They feel smart. While it's not smart to tell you, they just might. Also, the homeowner who has owned his house for many years likely has built up considerable equity by paying off his mortgage and gaining some appreciation. These sellers may be a bit more flexible in taking a slightly lower offer.

   However, if the sellers purchased their home anytime between 2005 and 2009, chances are, that house has lost value. They are not happy about it and, whatever their reasons for selling, they are already very frustrated at having to sell at a loss. The sellers are already losing money and will push very hard not to lose any more.

4. **If it is bank owned, how long has the property been vacant?** This is important information to have, because it will give you a very good idea of the condition of the house. If it has been sitting empty for more than thirty days, there is a good chance it has not been maintained properly. The systems may be in disrepair, maintenance may have been deferred, and items from the house may actually be missing or damaged.

5. **How do you like the neighborhood?** Unless there is gang graffiti on a burned-out house next door, the homeowners will tell you it's a nice neighborhood. But this question opens the door for you to query further about barking dogs, loud neighbors, kids repairing cars in the street, etc. Hopefully, they will be honest and give you a realistic picture of the neighborhood's character. Have there been any crimes committed nearby? Whatever the answer, probe further, and ask about house or car break-ins, petty thefts, or police activity. Obviously, this is important information.

6. **How old is the roof?** This can be a tough one to get answered. A cagey seller may say, "I'm not sure; I just know it doesn't leak." The correct follow-up is, "In the time you have owned the house, have you put on a new roof?" And if not, then ask if they have a contact number for the former owner. If they have owned the house more than fifteen years, you are getting close to needing a replacement. Most composite shingle roofs have a fifteen- to twenty-year life span. Tile or slate roofs last much longer. You would eventually find all this out in an inspection, but if you can find out now you may save yourself an expense. A new roof is a big cost, and if money is tight after having scraped together your down payment and closing costs, you may not want to be hit with a $6,000 to $10,000 repair bill during your first year in the house. You may need to keep shopping.

7. **When was the last time the furnace or heating system was cleaned and serviced?** The correct answer is "Once a season." What it tells you beyond the obvious state of the furnace is the kind of attention the seller has given to overall upkeep of the house and systems.

8. **What is your deadline to sell?** If the sellers are on a timetable, it can work to your advantage. They may want a short closing or a long one. They may want to sell the house because they need the money, but need to stay and rent back because of work or the school calendar. Or, conversely, they may prefer a long escrow in order to avoid taxes by hitting a certain date. Knowing to offer that rent-back can be a powerful negotiating tool.

9. **What's the one thing you won't miss about this house?** This is an open-ended question that can prompt the owners to share something they shouldn't. Asked casually, it can yield a piece of the truth that you can use to your advantage, either as a negotiating tool or as a basis for walking away.

10. **The Seller's Bottom Line: What Would You Take If I Gave You All Cash?** Okay, unless you're swimming in cash, you aren't going to be able to make an all-cash offer. But by

asking this question, your Realtor can learn a lot about the seller's flexibility and maybe even find out his or her bottom line. If the answer is "The asking price" followed by "Take it or leave it," then the seller is obviously not motivated.

 BYB Tip: How to Read Your Seller's Mind

I *always* ask my Realtor to "have a chat" with the selling broker *prior* to making an offer. Realtors will often resist this because it's extra work for them and sometimes a bother, but trust me, it will save you thousands!

Insist that your Realtor have a nice conversation with the seller's agent to find out as much as he can about the house's market history, the ten questions listed above, and what kinds of deal points the seller will respond to favorably. Your Realtor should then close the conversation with, "So, if I can get my buyer to write an offer, what do you think will get your seller to accept?"

As there is no written offer on the table, a selling agent is under fewer obligations of privacy and may reveal quite a bit more information than he or she can once an offer is on paper. You can now customize your offer. This is like having the answers to a test! You have just eliminated at least one round of offers and counteroffers, and you are guaranteed not to offer more than is necessary, possibly saving you tens of thousands.

Uncover the Financials—Condos and Co-ops

Depending upon your state or county, not all of a condo or co-op's financials are required to be presented or made available to you until you have an accepted offer. That does not mean you cannot ask ahead of time. Because when it comes to determining the value of a condo or co-op, getting the big picture of the building's financial health is critical.

As we discussed back in chapter 6, if you can, you will want to review the financials of a building before you make an offer. You will want to know all the monthly costs for each unit, any pending assessments, and especially any previously discussed future assessments. You will also want to know if the association has a respectable reserve fund in case of an emergency.

> ### ☑ BYB Tip: Within These Walls
>
> Ask your lawyer or real estate agent to examine the building documents to determine whether you own the walls of your unit or just the space between those walls. This sounds rather silly, but when you're battling over who pays for a broken water main in one of the walls, it's going to be important information to have. If you only own the space between your walls, then the broken pipe is the condo association's responsibility.

Get the Neighborhood Scoop

Chat up the neighbors. People love to small-talk and share . . . and, let's face it—gossip. If you are friendly and respectful, all you have to do is walk down the street and engage the neighbors to find out a wealth of information. Tell them you're thinking about buying the house, and since you're a potential neighbor, they'll be sizing you up, too, creating some common conversational ground. Ask how long they've lived there, how they like it, etc. With very little prodding, they will tell you about everything from messy divorces to the mall that's going in next year to barking dogs.

And a word about condos: While you are at the building, try to strike up a conversation in the lobby or out front with other owners. I can promise you, if there is a problem with one of the items listed below, you will hear about it after a few "neighborly" chats. Ask about:

- The board members
- The developer who built the building
- The other neighbors on your floor

Three Times Is the Charm

I like to see an interesting property at least three times before I make an offer: during the day to see the activity on the street, at rush hour to check for traffic, and at night to observe the noise and sense of safety.

While my editor was house shopping recently, she told me that her husband would refuse to consider ever buying a property or moving into a neighborhood until he walked the block on a warm summer night. That's when people are out on their porch or stoop or hanging around the front yard. What a great way to check out your prospective neighbors.

Getting the Scoop Gone Wrong—They Bark All Night

I bought a wonderful home in the Hollywood Hills. Unfortunately for me, it was the one time I did not follow my own advice to shoot the breeze with the neighbors to learn about potential problems. And my lack of due diligence caused me many sleepless nights—literally. My first night in the house, I woke to the sounds of two barking, yelping dogs that howled and bellowed until morning. I couldn't believe it. The next night the same thing happened. I later found out that the seller had been fighting with the neighbor over the barking dogs for six months, but never disclosed that to me. The surrounding neighbors had also been complaining, but the owners of the dogs just didn't care. It took me more than a year of working with Los Angeles Animal Control before the owners agreed to take responsibility for the problem. Had I chatted up neighbors sooner, I would have been much less tired all year long!

How Much Is That House Really Worth?

You know everything there is to know about your prospective dream house now. You have a basic idea of what this house has to offer, and you think you have a general sense of what might be wrong, fixable, or need work. You hope. You know why the seller is selling, and you know if the neighborhood is a good one.

But just because the sellers have decided to put it on the market for $425,000, is it really worth that? Is there any way to know what you should *really* be paying for this house? How much should you offer?

Well, you can't know for sure, but you can get a pretty darn good idea. There are two key factors that will determine if the price the seller is asking is in line with the house's worth—or just plain out of line.

How Much It Is Really Worth Depends on Two Factors

- The comps

- The temperature of the market

Comps + Temperature of the Market = House Value = Price

What Are the Comps and Why Are They Important?

Next to knowing all the seller's secrets, the comps—"comparables"—are you and your Realtor's most useful buying tool. By reviewing the comps with your agent, you can compare the prices of similar houses that are currently and have been recently on the market. Once you are able to surmise what your potential new house is really worth, you'll have a pretty clear indication of how much or how little of a discount you can expect from what the seller is asking.

Evaluating the Comps—the Elements of the Comps

- Apples to apples
- Asking price vs. sales price

Compare Apples to Apples

When analyzing the comps, you and your Realtor will need to find the houses that are an apples-to-apples match to your house candidate. You will want to put your potential new house head to head with the other houses that are on the market today or have sold recently by comparing the following features:

- **Square footage.** This is significant for most buyers. Some buyers will hunt for homes based on square footage alone. And when it comes to pricing, a bigger house means a bigger price.

- **Number of bedrooms and baths.** The number of bedrooms and baths can radically change the price of a home. Like square footage, families often shop for homes based on these numbers.

- **Amenities.** Obviously, the more amenities there are—such as a pool, spa, walk-in closets, gourmet kitchen, and so on—the higher the price.

- **Lot size.** Is there room to add on to the house or put in a pool? Or to plant a sprawling rose garden in the backyard? Is the house next door only spitting distance away? The exact acreage of the land correlates to price. When you compare this home to others, stay within .05 acres.

- **Age of the home.** Is this house new construction or a Victorian built in 1910? Or is the house relatively new, say, circa 1997? Of course, older homes don't necessarily command cheaper prices or vice versa, but you should try to compare like to like.

- **Condition.** When you compare the home to others, consider the condition. Whether it's a fixer-upper, a teardown, completely updated, or pristine, the condition of the house can be a deal maker or deal breaker and a major factor when comparing house to house.

- **Location.** This factor is multifaceted. It relates not only to your state, city, and neighborhood, but also to where the house sits on the street and in what part of your neighborhood. Is it near a freeway or busy intersection? And a great tip from Peter Pasternack of TLC's show *Flip This House* is triple-check that the houses you compare are not across county lines—no matter how close by.

BYB Tip: Keep It Local

It's very important to remember that real estate is incredibly local. Often the message found in a national news headlines may have little to do with conditions locally in your specific area. When it comes to home prices, microeconomic climates exist across many parts of the country; home prices can be slowly rising or holding steady, or softening . . . all at the same time. That is why it's so important to focus on comps locally. Price is always relative to locale.

Asking Prices vs. Sale Prices: The Temperature of the Market

The asking price of a house currently on the market is just that— the *asking* price. It is not what the house is really worth. So don't be fooled by looking at only the asking prices of houses on the market. You must look at the prices of what has sold. You get a much more valid idea of pricing by examining what has recently *sold* rather than what is currently *for sale.*

Knowing the percentage difference between the actual list and sale prices for the houses in your neighborhood is invaluable. It speaks volumes about the current market's activity. This is a strong indicator of which direction the market is moving, and it will indicate how much less, or maybe even more, than the asking price you should offer.

In other words, if the comps show that several houses in that neighborhood were listed around $500,000 but sold later for $450,000, you know that you might want to make an offer that is 10 percent lower than what the seller is currently asking. In a hot market, if those same houses that were listed at $500,000 had sold for $550,000, then you would know that you might need to pay as much as 10 percent over the current asking price.

Generally speaking, if the percentage differences for homes that sold are between −5 and −10 percent, you're in a soft market. Sellers aren't getting what they think their homes are worth. And they probably aren't selling their homes as quickly as they'd like. If the percentage differences are between −10 and −20 percent—or more—the

List vs. Sale Price Comparison		
List Price	Sale Price	Difference (%)
$180,000	$159,000	−12%
$420,000	$405,000	−4%
$1,200,000	$1,350,000	13%
$799,000	$650,000	−19%
$385,000	$400,000	4%

market is extremely weak. Of course, if those percentages are positive, then you're in a warm, potentially hot market and sellers are getting multiple offers over asking price.

What's This House Worth Today, Not Tomorrow?

Just like in life, it's great to be appreciated. It's wonderful when those around you appreciate you. But any therapist or professional will tell you, the key to personal success is when your self-esteem and value as a person are not dependent on others' appreciation. The same holds true for real estate. When you buy a house without depending on appreciation, you will be successful regardless of other market forces, or what the market itself is doing.

New Rule: Don't Bank On Market Appreciation

Don't overpay and expect the market to bail you out. A huge home-buyer's mistake in the recent downturn was to overpay, expecting the market would save you with the kind of astronomical instant appreciation we saw in 2002–2006. Nope, it's not going to happen again. Sure, there will be long-term market appreciation, but the kind of short-term growth we saw back then—sorry! You must make sure the numbers work even if market prices do *not* increase in the short run. Make sure you only pay based on what the house is worth today—not what it will be worth next year or five years down the line.

I often tell students at my seminars that back in 2002–2006, almost everyone was able to make money in real estate. You had to *try* to lose money in those years. The battle cry of the ill-informed then was "If we overpay or overimprove, the market will bail us out." However, when the market cycle spun downward, all those over-zealous and uneducated homebuyers and even investors were badly burned.

Appreciation is the bonus, but never count on it! You will never miscalculate if you assume there will be *no* appreciation. You will always be pleasantly surprised. So when trying to determine your offer price, it's critical to determine a home's real worth today—not bank on what it will be worth tomorrow.

 BYB Tip: Doesn't Matter What They Paid for It

Remember, don't make the mistake of basing a home's worth, and thus the price you offer, on what the current owners paid for their property. Although knowing what they originally paid can help you figure out how motivated they are to sell based on their equity, that old purchase price has nothing to do with where we are in today's market. Value has nothing to do with a previous sale's price if real estate prices have escalated or descended since that purchase.

What You Learned in This Chapter

♦ Before you make an offer on a house, you need to find out as much about both the house and the seller as you can.

♦ It's important to know how long the house has been on the market and if there have been any other offers. This will give you a great indication of the seller's flexibility on price.

♦ How much a house is *really* worth depends on two key components: the comps of similar houses and the temperature of the market.

♦ When determining a house's value, it's imperative to look at the prices of houses that have recently sold as well as the prices of houses currently on the market.

♦ Don't overpay and expect the market appreciation to bail you out. Analyze your offer price for the price of the house today—not what you think it will be worth tomorrow.

CHAPTER 11

Writing the House-Winning Offer

When buying a house, at the most fundamental level, one person wants to sell, and one person wants to buy. Once the terms are agreed upon, voilà . . . win-win. However, if one party is miserable with the final terms, no one wins. The deal will ultimately fall apart, unravel, or turn ugly, causing you aggravation and costing you time and money in the end.

Creating the Win-Win Deal—It's All about Integrity

Integrity in real estate, business, and life is a smart mantra to live by. People want to deal with people who are honest and share similar values. I'm a big believer that all deals can be win-win for everyone when integrity is the underlying code of behavior. This is particularly true when making an offer on a house.

My point is that your good deal should not be based on someone else's loss. When you act, offer, and negotiate with honesty and integrity, everyone wins—especially you.

So keep in mind, as you begin the deal-making stage of home buying, that honesty is the best policy. Try to come to a fair and equitable agreement; negotiate strong but by all means treat everyone in the negotiation with respect and honor. You will be very surprised at how positively sellers, agents, lawyers, and all the other players involved will respond to that. These principles have worked for me and they will work for you, too.

Don't Buy Emotionally

I know by this point in the process you are crazy in love with this home you have found and want to buy. You now know a lot about the seller and details of the property, and you have been to see it hopefully more than twice. You have been decorating it in your mind and you have been visualizing your furniture in each of the rooms already. That little alcove where the hat rack goes was so cute. The way the sun shone through the master bedroom window was inspiring. You are really into it. You are hooked. You must have it, right?

Remember: Don't Love It Too Much

Danger! Danger! You are right now about to psyche yourself into the most vulnerable and powerless bargaining position possible. You have now become an emotional buyer. You are now the buyer that sellers and sellers' agents dream about.

 BYB Buyer's Blunder: Getting Too Attached to the House

You must remember that it's just a house. There will be others. Make your best offer, play it out, but don't ever get too attached. The key to negotiating from a position of strength is being willing to walk away. When buyers get too emotionally attached to a house, it's *over*. They overpay on price, overlook issues, and overextend their home-buying budget—all huge mistakes. There's another dream house out there, but if you're stuck on the one that got away, you'll miss your opportunity to find the ideal house for you today.

Yes, you are buying a home for the innumerable ways it will enrich your lifestyle. Yes, it needs to be your nesting place and the home you have always longed for. Nevertheless, remember that it is an investment first and you need to select it with that in mind. When chosen correctly and purchased properly, it can become the nest egg and financial safety net that you will rely upon in coming years. Choosing solely based on your emotions is a foolish business plan. Would you select a stock just because you liked its name, or the way its logo looked on the Web site? Of course not; you select a stock based on its strength, performance, and affordability. A house is a far bigger investment than a few stocks, so why would you not put a house through the same examination as you do your stocks?

The Secret to Counteract a *Ready, Set, Sold!* Seller

In my book *Ready, Set, Sold! The Insider Secrets to Sell Your House Fast—for Top Dollar!* I teach sellers that the way to squeeze top dollar out of buyers is to grab them emotionally. In all of my real estate lecturing and writing, I explain to sellers that "buyers buy *emotionally*, not *intellectually*." Emotional buyers overpay for houses!

Well, not you. You are not going to fall prey to the tricks and traps of the well-read seller. You are going to win the home-buying game by keeping your emotions at bay like a professional. Don't let your emotions sabotage smart business decisions. Buy with your head, not your heart, and you will pay less and buy smart—even when faced with the most savvy and tough negotiating sellers.

Three Steps to the Offer Process

There are many names for sales contracts across the country. Even though they're called something different across state lines, no matter what the name—purchase offer, purchase and sales agreement, contract of sale, agreement of sale, land contract, binder, and so on—they all accomplish the same thing. They are temporary "agreements" that intend to bind the buyer and seller to basic terms until either escrow is opened or a lawyer drafts a full purchase agreement and puts the deal under contract. Minor variations aside, the one feature they have in common, however, is the three steps to the offer process.

Three Steps to the Offer Process

1. Putting the Offer Together
2. Presenting the Offer
3. The Counteroffer

Offer Step 1: Putting the Offer Together

The offer. It sounds like a big deal but it is nothing more than a starting point that includes the price you want to pay, the contingencies that must be met, the terms, the deposit, and the down payment. All of these elements can be finessed to create a win-win situation if you learn to use them as bargaining chips. Your goal is to make an offer that is irresistible, yet at the price you want and the terms with which you are comfortable.

By the way, it's not all about the price. Well, sure, a big price tag is the first thing that every seller wants to see. But any good Realtor will advise his seller that every offer is a sum of its parts. And if you understand all of the five components that go into an offer, you may be able to put together a winning offer at a lower price.

1. Price

Indeed, price is the most critical component of your offer. So you need to put a lot of consideration into how much you offer, and how you offer it. This is a dance between you and the seller that could go on for two or even three rounds of offers and counteroffers.

Determining your offer price is where your sleuthing and information gathering in the last chapter really pays off. Knowing the motivation of the seller, any previous offers, what the house is really worth, and any hidden costs, will help you zero in on that perfect offer price.

Do you offer the asking price, do you offer lower—how much lower? Or should you offer higher than asking right from the get-go? Having analyzed the comps, you and your Realtor have determined

The Five Components to Any Offer

1. Price
2. Deposit
3. Down payment
4. Contingencies
   —Inspection
   —Disclosures
   —Financing
   —Appraisal
   —Clear Title
5. Terms
   —Length of Closing
   —Choice of Escrow, Closing, Settlement and Title Companies
   —Home Warranty
   —Closing Costs
   —Right to Assign
   —Personal Property
   —Terms of Possession

the temperature of the market, which now helps you finalize that magic offer number. So is there a method to the best offer strategy? Yes, there is. Keep in mind that you can always increase your offer price, but you really can't decrease it.

Lowballing Doesn't Really Get You the Deals

Okay, I really want to talk about this. I was on a morning talk show, and we were discussing the real estate market and the best way to shop for a home, and also the best way to win the deal. The overzealous and somewhat cocky host said, "Well, I like to just throw the offers out there and really *lowball* them!" I paused for a moment and said, "How's that working for you?" He admitted that he has actually not been able to get sellers to meet him halfway, and oftentimes they don't even respond.

When people sell their homes, they are selling a piece of themselves. This house is the setting of someone's life. For the seller, its value includes what it represents, not just what it lists for. Lowballing, while it sounds like a great way to get a cheap deal, can get you off on the wrong foot. When you are clearly lowballing, a seller and a good seller's agent are not going to take you seriously. In fact, even if they do respond at all, that seller now emotionally does not want to sell you the house and will do anything to encourage another buyer to step up, so that they don't have to deal with you.

Be smart. Be reasonable with your initial offer. You may not even get a chance to negotiate if you've offended the other party out of playing the game. It is always best to submit an offer that could possibly be something the owner would consider. The best-case scenario is that you submit an offer, the owner counters back midway between your offer and the asking price, and you then agree. Done. Win-win.

 BYB Buyer's Blunder: Lowballing Gone Wrong

In my early days of buying homes, my Realtor called me about a cute little 1920s Craftsman house in Hollywood that was about to go on the market at $303,000. It was a fixer, and at that price, it was a very good deal. Well, I thought, okay, I'll pay $303,000, but first I want to see if I can lowball and get it for less. My Realtor warned me not to lowball, but I offered $270,000, figuring they would come back and close the deal at $290,000. Well, they did, but with someone who came in right at $290,000. They were so offended by my low offer that they refused to sell it to me at any price! My Realtor reminds me of this story today!

---

2. Deposit

A deposit is not the same thing as a down payment. Deposits are submitted to show that you're a serious buyer who intends to make this purchase happen. Though sometimes they are not required, good-faith deposits are usually between 3 and 6 percent of the purchase price, depending on what's standard in your area. Your Realtor will know what's typical for your location. This money is typically held by a neutral third party, such as an escrow company, and it is credited back to you on the day you close or it becomes part of the down payment. And if the deal falls through, there are some cases when the seller is entitled to keep your deposit. There is always a risk with putting up a deposit. So, here are three ways you can help mitigate your risk.

1. **Put up a smaller deposit.** Some states have suggested or contracted deposits of 3 percent.

2. **Increase your deposit later.** Make a smaller initial deposit but include language that states you'll increase it once the contingencies are all met and removed.

3. **Write the check, hold the funds.** Make the offer with the caveat that the deposit check will not be cashed at least until the sellers accept your offer.

3. Down Payment

As we discussed earlier in great detail, the least amount of money I suggest you put down is 20 percent, for all the reasons reviewed in chapter 2. But here's one more. When it comes to landing the deal, many sellers feel that the bigger the down payment, the more financially able the buyer. Although this is not necessarily true, if there is competition for the house you like—especially in a multiple-bidding situation—this posture can make you more attractive. It makes you a stronger buying candidate than someone trying to buy that same house with anything less.

4. Contingencies

Contingencies are negotiating tools that can be used with great success. They give you an opportunity to walk away without consequence. The most common contingencies are the inspection, the disclosures, and then the mortgage contingencies. If you don't like what you see at the inspection or in the seller's disclosures, which we will discuss in chapter 13, or if you can't get the mortgage at the terms you need, you have the right to take your deposit back and move on.

These contingencies are often thought of as escape clauses for buyers. They are a buyer's solid backup plan for backing out. In fact, when the market was peaking in the mid-2000s, aggressive buyers would make offers on properties they had not even seen in order to tie them up, knowing they could use these contingencies to walk away.

Contingencies are an important safeguard. But use them judiciously, keeping as many in as possible without loading down the offer.

Contingent upon Inspection

You hire a licensed inspector to inspect your property. He puts together a report. After your inspection, you give the seller your list of problems, current and potential, along with the opportunity to fix them, make a price adjustment, or give you a credit back. If the seller does not agree to any of your requests, you can walk.

As the buyer, the burden is on you to have your inspection and present your list in a timely manner. There is always a standard number of days allotted to complete your inspection. Otherwise, you waive the right to this particular contingency. We will be discussing the best way to make the most of the inspections and this negotiating opportunity in chapter 13.

Contingent upon Disclosures

As we will discuss in chapter 13, by law the seller has to fill out a seller's disclosure statement about all known defects. If you don't like what you see on the statement, you can walk away from the deal.

Contingent upon Financing

Another opportunity to walk away from the deal is if you can't get the financing you want. Not only are you off the hook, but you also get your deposit back. Unless you are paying all cash for this house, you should always make an offer with a loan contingency.

With most thirty- to forty-five-day closings, you will usually have seventeen to twenty-one days to get your mortgage approval. You don't have to alert the seller that your mortgage is finalized and approved until the final day of your contingency period. But if it is looking like your mortgage is held up or not forthcoming, as is often the case in today's market, make sure you don't miss your deadline to jump ship or ask for an extension of the contingency.

BYB Tip: Use the Mortgage Terms to Keep You In or Out of the Deal

Especially when interest rates are rising, pay close attention to the interest rate you agree to accept in the contract. Always include an interest rate and a cap on the total mortgage points that are as low as possible. In other words, if you will not be comfortable paying a 6 percent rate plus 1 point on your loan, put 5.5 percent as the top rate and one-half point to pay. This gives you leeway to get out of the deal if your lender can't get you the loan within your comfort zone. And it keeps a tight cap on the terms to which you agree.

Contingent upon Appraisal

In today's market, the downward shift in home prices, coupled with the number of foreclosures being sold off, has resulted in changes to appraisals. It's very possible that the house may not appraise for what you have offered to pay. If that is the case, you will want to have the option to walk away. While appraisal contingencies have not been very common in the past, they are gaining popularity. Fran Broude of Coldwell Banker Residential in Chicago advises that buyers who are putting a large deposit down or are paying all cash should include an appraisal contingency as an added safeguard.

Contingent upon Clear Title

"Clear title" is a term I will explain in chapter 15. This contingency basically allows the buyer to walk with no penalty if the seller cannot prove that he or she is the actual owner of the house, and that there will be no other loans or liens against the property at the time of closing. This one is pretty standard and often already written into most sales agreement forms.

Too Many versus Not Enough Contingencies

Every contingency that you add has the potential to make your offer look weaker because it makes it that much harder to close the deal. Lawyer-negotiated deals can get loaded with contingencies very fast. Lighten up and make sure you really want what you're asking for. Otherwise your seller may look elsewhere. However, I would never recommend a sales contract with no contingencies even in the hottest, most competitive markets. You take a huge risk when you offer a contract with no contingencies. And as you know by now, I am all about buying safe and sane. I like fallback options and exit plans.

Contingent on the Sale of the Buyer's Own Home

Here's one more. But this is one I *don't* recommend. Making the *purchase* of this new house contingent on the *sale* of your house is a huge red flag for sellers, especially in today's market. Let's be realistic, your sellers can barely get their own house sold, and now you are asking them to worry if *your* house will sell before you can buy theirs? Most sellers will say no to this. And it makes your offer to buy their home look pretty lame and shaky.

 BYB Tip: Stretch Contingencies Out as Long as Possible

Your goal as a buyer is to push for longer contingency periods and to tie your seller up in the deal as quickly as possible. This is the opposite strategy that I teach to home *sellers*, so let's just hope that your sellers have not taken one of my home-selling seminars or read my previous books. You want to ask for a long contingency period to stretch out as long as possible the number of days you have to "escape" without penalty. This gives you the ability to walk away from the deal until the last possible moment.

5. Terms

The terms pretty much cover all the other possible elements and negotiable aspects of the deal, from how long it will take to close, to who gets the refrigerator.

Length of Escrow

The time it takes to close the deal—the length of escrow—can vary. Escrow is generally thirty, forty-five, sixty, or ninety days. Escrow terms can be one of the great negotiating tools. Customizing the length of escrow to suit the seller's needs can often seal the deal with a lower-priced offer. A seller will generally want a fast closing, usually thirty days. If you have all your ducks in a row, you may be able to do this—and snag yourself a lower price in the process.

This is where getting all the dirt will come in handy again. Maybe the sellers need to move right away. Perhaps they have to hold the property until a certain date for tax reasons, but want the security of knowing the property is already sold. Or maybe the house they are moving to won't be ready for sixty days. Find out what they need, then give it to them. It makes your offer look good and costs you nothing. If you have some flexibility and are not in a situation that is forcing you to relocate and move immediately, then use the length of escrow as a negotiating tactic.

Choice of Escrow, Closing, Settlement, and Title Companies

Depending on where in the country you are, you will have to make a choice about who will handle your closing. Your Realtor will have favorites because every Realtor has a relationship with an escrow or settlement office and a title company. Name your own choice in the offer; however, a good negotiating ploy is to let the seller have his pick—providing you get something in exchange in the counteroffer.

I'll discuss the details of escrow and title companies in the next chapter. You may not even have to deal with these entities if your state does the closing dance a little differently. But most sales do encounter title companies to some degree—or at least their attorneys who are handling the closing do.

Home Warranty Policy

This is a wonderful way of getting some protection from the seller that ensures the systems, appliances, plumbing, and electrical wiring in the house are working and operational. You could consider coming up in price if the seller offers to buy you this policy for a year, which is approximately $500. Ask for it in your initial offer, knowing you can pull it off the table in counteroffers for something in return! We'll talk more about the value of this insurance-like coverage in chapter 15.

Closing Costs

"Who pays what" is another opportunity for flexibility, and it gives you some negotiating room in an upcoming counter situation. Certain states already have standard practices in place as to who pays what, but it never hurts to ask, especially in a counteroffer or multiple-offer situation. Sometimes fees for title, escrow, and county or city transfer taxes can equal 1 to 2 percent of the sales price.

Right to Assign

You want the right to assign the contract if you so choose, as the buyer. This means that if you wanted to, you would be allowed to add your name as buyer with "and/or assigns." You could then sell off this great deal to someone else before you even close, if you choose. If there is language in the contract that forbids assignment without the seller's permission, then cross it out. If you are a first-time homebuyer or you are truly buying this house to move into, this clause may not be important and you do not have to include it. However, if you are an investor and there is a chance that you have scooped up this house for a great price and want to sell it to someone else even before you close, then you will want to have this option open to you.

Personal Property

It is best to add in your requests for personal property now. Do you want the appliances included? Is that aboveground hot tub in the backyard something you want? Is it *really*? Are you in love with that chandelier in the entryway and want to make sure it is still hanging there on sale day? You need to make a notation in the contract.

Word to the wise, this is not an opportunity to play supermarket sweep. Be very selective about what you ask for. Submitting a two-page list of additional items to the seller is going to turn them off and sour them. Remember, it's stressful enough selling off their home; don't start picking through their furnishings even before you have a deal. Try to keep it to appliances and fixtures.

Terms of Possession: It's Mine Now—or Is It?

Finally—this may sound silly, but it's a biggie and a lot of great home sales turn ugly at the last minute over this one. And it's so simple to prevent. Just be specific about possession. Possession is the day and time that the buyers have full possession and the ability to actually move in if they choose. That means the sellers will be moved out. Spell out the possession date. Is it on closing day? A day after closing?

BYB Tip: Watch the Wording

It's to your advantage to have a "liquidated damages" clause in your sales contract. This clause offers some extra protection for you. It basically means that if for some reason you back out after your contingencies expire or without just cause, the sellers can't sue you for damages because they instead get to keep your deposit. Not all of these clauses are worded the same way or mean the same thing. Consult with your Realtor or attorney to make sure it's worded in your favor.

Offer Step 2: Presenting the Offer

Okay, it's all ready to go. You have the price you want to offer decided upon, the offer paperwork is all neatly filled out, and your Realtor is ready to call the selling agent to say "We have an offer." But wait, there are a few more things you need to consider before he drives on over, e-mails it, or even faxes it to the selling agent.

The Two Dream Buyer Letters

In addition to the offer itself, there are two letters to include in your offer that will make you a dream buyer to any seller. One is a window on your financial picture that demonstrates your creditworthiness. The other is a window on your soul that proves that no one could appreciate this beautiful home more than you.

The Two Dream Buyer Letters

- The Letter of Preapproval
- The "Please Let Me Buy Your House" Letter

The Letter of Preapproval

As we discussed in chapter 4, "Getting Your Credit in Order," the preapproval letter you acquired from your mortgage broker or bank when you started looking is now going to be put to use. Being pre-approved by a mortgage broker for a set amount truly puts your best financial foot forward. It means that the lender preapproves you for a loan, in essence turning you into a cash buyer. And as mortgages are harder to come by these days, it is your all-access pass to a fast deal—because you are good to go.

The "Please Let Me Buy Your House" Letter

I know, I know, you are thinking this is soooo cheesy. But let me share a story and then you decide for yourself. A professional real estate investor friend of mine, who specializes in flipping, had his house on the market. The house went into multiple offers with three similar offers on the table. Two of the offers came with very heartfelt letters explaining how much the potential buyers liked the house, would love to live in the neighborhood, loved the view, etc. Even though my friend is a seasoned professional, he was actually put off by the buyer who *didn't* send a letter because the others did—and he sold to one of the letter writers. The moral is to write a sincere letter about who you are and to highlight the qualities about the house you really like. They may never read it, but they sure will take note that you wrote it.

Put a Time Limit on Signing

A selling agent likes to take his time presenting an incoming offer to his client because the longer it takes, the longer he has to tell other potential buyers, "There's an offer on the table—it may go into a multiple-offer situation—so you had better sweeten your offer." Thus, if a seller lets your offer sit without responding immediately, he or she may be waiting for a better one.

It's always best to include a deadline for acceptance and "Expiration of Offer" in the offer. Set a twenty-four-hour deadline in which the seller must act, either to accept, reject, or counter your offer. It forces him or her to do something or lose you as a buyer. It's up to your agent to know the difference between a seller that's stalling and a seller who happens to be on vacation.

Offer Step 3: The Counteroffer

So you and your Realtor put together what you feel is a pretty good offer. You think you have offered a fair and reasonable amount of money and terms your sellers will be happy with. But, arggh, the sellers didn't just sign on the dotted line and say, "Take it—it's yours!" What? Really? They didn't? What do you mean they want to counter back?

The offer process is full of opportunities to incrementally improve your position. From the very first offer to the counteroffer to the inspection, every shift is a chance for more solid footing. I never take no for an answer. I always come back with a way to keep the ball in play. In my experience, there is always a way to amend, add to, increase, or tweak an offer while keeping it a win-win for everyone.

Buying a house is all about negotiating and making offers. In fact, it happens three different times. First when you put together and presented your initial offer. Now as you receive and respond back to a counteroffer. And then, if you do get an accepted offer, you'll have one last negotiating opportunity after you complete your house inspection. The third opportunity, after your inspection, is going to be a bit more involved of a dance. Chapter 13, "The House Inspection," will give you all the right moves.

The Counteroffer Back

The seller's counteroffer has been presented to your Realtor. As he or she is reviewing it with you, you are annoyed; you take it personally. You might even say, "But I wrote that really nice note to them telling them why I want to buy their house." Well, once again, I say *calm down.* Take a deep breath. Take your emotions out of it. This is all part of the process.

Most, if not all, sellers will be advised to counter back. The counter back may be for a lot more money than what you have offered, or simply a counter back about some of the terms. And it might be just to counter back at their original asking price with no movement in your direction at all. But no matter what it is, just know that countering is a normal function of this business. In fact, you should be very suspicious if they don't counter back!

Counteroffer Success

Countering is an art. Now is the time to put your business hat on and drive a hard bargain. When considering a counteroffer, try to look at it from a wholly positive perspective—even when it's less than perfect. Remember that there are many creative ways of coming out a winner.

The first step in countering is evaluating exactly what it is about the seller's offer that isn't good enough for you. List what's unacceptable.

> The trick to successful negotiating is accentuating the positive and trying to gradually improve the negative.

Walking through the five components of the offer will allow you to review all of your seller's counteroffer components and then structure your counteroffer without missing a single item. Go back to the list at the beginning of this chapter and make sure each item is either agreed upon or addressed. If your seller wants you to pump up your offer price, instead maybe you can make the closing timeline more appealing. Then decide on what you're going to request in order to turn those unacceptables into acceptables.

Let's face it. Most of the focus of the back-and-forth will be about the price. But as we are discussing here, this is the time to utilize all the other components of the offer to get you closer to the win-win deal at the price you want.

Negotiating the Counteroffer

The Essential Dos and Don'ts of Negotiating the Counteroffer

- DO take your emotions out of the equation.

- DO counter back, always. Keep the game going.

- DO be willing to make *some* sacrifices—especially if you find the perfect house and are hung up only on minor issues.

- DO know what your bottom-line price is, above which you will walk away from the deal.

- DO try to adjust your demands for terms. Be creative and try to find ways to compromise the price versus the deal savers.

- DO respond quickly. Remember that in counteroffers time is *not* your friend—get it wrapped up quickly. Create as many strict deadlines as possible. Time limits for the sellers to respond show that you are serious. Don't give the sellers more than twelve to twenty-four hours to accept, counter, or reject your counteroffer.

- DON'T expect verbal agreements to work in real estate.

- DO present your counteroffers in writing. Keep all changes, modifications, and deadline extensions in writing.

- DO keep your paperwork orderly and organized. Make sure all addenda and counters are properly numbered and attached appropriately.

- DON'T get greedy! If you can live with your seller's offer, accept it. Haggling over minor odds and ends can kill your deal—and you! And get this: if your seller offers you a deal very close to your offer price, the back-and-forth of more counteroffers may only aggravate your seller. Don't forget you will have another chance to negotiate a better position after your inspection.

Time now to put it in writing, sign the form, and get it back to the seller for review. If he or she signs it—sold! If it comes back to you with a new offer, you'll have to repeat the process, hopefully inching you closer to a final deal.

Eleventh-Hour Deal Savers

You're countering back and forth; maybe now you're in round two of the counteroffers. The sellers are still a tad too high for your checkbook, but you are getting so very close. It seems like you are at a stalemate over silly things and very little money. It happens all the time. Sometimes the sellers really dig their heels in on the price. Yes, it is slightly more than you want to pay. What can you do? Here are some other ideas to consider if you're in the throes of negotiating and you need that extra little push to get the deal signed off.

- **Ask the sellers to pay your closing costs.** You may offer to pay their asking price if they pick up the fees for the closing costs. For most buyers, especially first-timers, the down payment is the biggest obstacle when buying a home. If you can get the sellers to pay those closing costs, that can be between 1.5 and 3 percent of your loan amount. This saves you a bundle and allows you to accept their current asking price in return.

- **Ask to raise the price.** What?! Yes, you read that correctly. If the sellers are not willing to kick in some of the closing costs outright, here's a another great deal saver, and a great way to stretch your down payment money a bit further. Ask the sellers to raise the price of the house. But in return you would then like them to pay your closing costs. This actually does not change the amount of money that the sellers receive at the time of the sale but it does reduce the money that you have to come up with for the closing.

- **Cover the inspection.** Ask them to pay for the home inspection and in return you'll come up a bit in price.

- **Ask the Realtors to kick in part of their commission as a credit for the cost of some of the above items.** Oftentimes, when the deal is close but not close enough, the selling Realtor will kick in the cost of the home warranty, or a credit from his commissions toward some of the closing costs for the buyer. Just as often, my Realtor will also get the seller's Realtor to match amounts—to double the credit back!

- **Offer to rent back.** Let's say your sellers really need a thirty-day escrow but they don't want to move to their new location that fast. This may be the one negotiating item that could seal the deal: close the deal in their requested thirty days but then *rent back* to the sellers until they are ready to move out. This is a great way for sellers to close the property, get their cash out of the sale, and have time to get ready to move.

The Backup Position—When Losing the Deal Can Be a Win

So you lost the house to someone else. You may never know why. Maybe they offered more money or their terms were slightly better than yours. But it's not all bad news; in fact, there may be a silver lining here. You can ask the seller to accept your offer as a backup offer. It costs you nothing. You don't have to put out any money, yet you are in line to get the property if the current buyer falls out. Plus, sellers love backup offers because it puts pressure on the accepted offerer to close the deal quickly, knowing that there is another buyer standing in the wings hoping to take center stage.

I have won big in backup situations where there has already been an inspection and the house falls out because there are problems that the buyer can't handle. Or simply because the buyer was not able to get his loan. In this situation, I have the advantage of jumping in to save the day when the seller is now frustrated and just wants to sell and get out. It puts me in a stronger negotiating position.

If you do find yourself in a backup position, there are four things to include in a backup offer.

Four Backup Offer Must-Haves

1. **Thirty-Day Time Limit**—Make your backup offer expire after thirty days. The longer the time it takes to complete the current transaction, the greater the chance the two parties have to work through their differences. A time limit will force the hand of your competition, which may make them unable to close the deal.

2. **Right of Refusal**—You're not bound to take the property, but once they've accepted your backup offer, they are bound to ask you first.

3. **Get the Terms in the Agreement in Writing**—Lock those sellers into you. Make sure that they are obligated to sell to you within a certain period of time at the agreed-upon terms if the property becomes available.

4. **Extra Bonus for the Backup Buyer**—Legally the sellers have to disclose any problems the first-position buyers uncovered, maybe even ones that made them bolt! As a result, you will know the property's recently uncovered flaws ahead of time.

Don't Buy the New House before You Sell the Old House

This may be your situation. You need to move, and you need to purchase a new home. You want to put an offer on a great new house but haven't sold your old one yet. Trying to buy the new house before you sell the old house can be a difficult balancing act, if not next to impossible in today's market. There is too much uncertainty and I advise against being "caught in between" two houses at all costs.

Sell your house first. Rent, then start shopping. It puts you in the power seat. You don't have a mortgage on an empty house hanging over your head, you have money in the bank, and you didn't have to sell your old house out of desperation and fear of carrying two mortgages. The last thing you want to do is find yourself in the position of having to become a desperate seller. Buyers smell blood when they know you have already bought a house and are really motivated to off-load your old one. I promise you, you will be receiving offers on your old house, but they will be lowballs under your asking price.

Yes, there are options if you get stuck, but my advice in today's market is . . . don't get stuck.

But where are we supposed to live in the meantime, you ask? Here are some ideas:

1. **Rent back from your buyer.** Sell your house first, close the deal, then rent it back from the new owners until your purchase transaction for a new home is completed. Coordinating a leaseback alleviates financial concerns and removes the hassle of having to go to a temporary residence before moving into a new home.

2. **Rent a place.** You may not always be able or willing to lease your old home, so renting a property is another option to

consider. Although relocating twice in quick succession is not ideal, renting serves as a fix for the short term. And it's also a good option if you need a place to hang your hat if you are planning some renovations to the house.

3. **Buy on contingency.** Have a prior-sale contingency included in the purchase contract for the new home. It provides the opportunity to withdraw an offer if your existing home does not sell by a certain date. Forewarning: very few but the most desperate sellers are going to agree to sell to you if you have this contingency in place.

4. **Get a bridge loan.** If you absolutely *have* to buy before you sell, consider a bridge loan. Bridge loans enable buyers to move forward with the purchase of a home while the current home remains on the market, by borrowing from the existing home's equity until the proceeds from its sale are obtained. Though some bridge loans can be extended if need be, they

> But my best piece of advice in today's market: don't buy until you sell.

can become extremely expensive if protracted. This is a risky choice, therefore if you must, it's best to use them for overlaps of a few days between closings or, at the most, a few weeks.

What You Learned in This Chapter

♦ Don't buy emotionally. This is one of the biggest financial expenditures you will ever make, so treat it as a business transaction.

♦ The price you offer is important, but there are five other components to consider that include terms, contingencies, and time.

♦ Contingencies are your escape clauses and even opportunities to renegotiate; make sure you include them in your offer.

♦ Lowballing doesn't really get you the best deal, and oftentimes it can close you out of the deal completely.

♦ From an emotional standpoint, never take a counteroffer personally; keep it all business. Just reanalyze and counter back by trying to accentuate the acceptable terms and mitigate the unacceptable terms of the deal.

♦ In today's market, avoid having to buy the new house before you sell the old.

PART FIVE

Closing

CHAPTER 12

You Have an Accepted Offer! Now What?

Congratulations, the seller has accepted your offer. But what does that mean? You make a couple of phone calls, tell the bank what kind of mortgage you'd like, write a check, sign on the dotted line, and get the key? Is it now all blue skies and green lights? Nope. I hate to break it to you but now the hardest work is about to begin. You are about to be inundated with phone calls, paperwork, inspection reports, faxes, notaries, and a profusion of questions and forms.

What Have I Done? The Big Freak-out!

This has been a very exciting and exhilarating process up to this point. You found a house, negotiated a deal you are comfortable with, you have opened escrow and turned in your deposit, and now all of a sudden . . . the reality hits. "Oh, my God, I am buying a house." That reality may be frightening, it may be paralyzing. You may be saying, "What have I done?!"

I'm happy to tell you that this is an absolutely normal experience. Almost every buyer goes through what we call buyer's remorse. It's completely natural and it will pass. But you need to understand why it comes up in the first place.

Let me share a little secret. I have bought and sold dozens of homes for myself and every single time I buy a house or property I have what some friends of mine referred to as "the Big Freak-out." My Realtor jokes with me about the fact that I put myself and my home purchase through an exhaustive reanalysis of the deal every time. Should I or shouldn't I? Do I really want this house? Is it a good deal? Have I made the right decision?

Fortunately, even though I allow myself a period of "meltdown" I am able to rely on my experience and practical approach to home buying to know that I have taken all the steps to seek, evaluate, analyze, and select the perfect property!

So go ahead, have a little moment, freak out, and indulge in some buyer's remorse. But when you are ready to work through the meltdown, here are five questions you need to ask to make sure you've made all the right moves. Once answered, these questions will allow you to know if this freak is going to put you out . . . or into this deal.

The Five Questions That Question Your Freak-out

1. Did you complete the three steps to house shopping? Did you start online, check out open houses, then seriously shop with a qualified Realtor?
2. Does this house hit most of your must-haves and should-haves on your Dream House Checklist?
3. Did you get all the dirt on this house? Did you find out about the house's history and the seller's needs?
4. Does the accepted purchase price of the house reflect the analysis you did of what the house is really worth? Did you review all the comps with your Realtor, looking at what has sold and what hasn't sold?
5. Most important, did you realistically examine your finances to determine that a house in this price range is one you can afford?

If you just answered yes to at least four of the five questions, then it's time to move forward with your purchase and feel confident that

you've made the right decision. Notice that each of these questions is
based on the *Before You Buy* step-by-
step strategies of smart home buying that I've been explaining thus
far. If you've been vigilant about
following all the steps, then you
should have some pretty darn strong
yes answers here.

> **Remember, in today's new market, an educated and well-informed buyer is a smart buyer. Smart buyers make smart decisions. You are now a smart buyer.**

Walking through the Closing Land Mines

Even before the ink is dry on the signatures of your accepted offer,
you need to be thinking about the closing process. The *escrow, closing,*
or *contract* period is everything that happens from the signing of the
agreement of sale to the final closing and cash-out.

Let me warn you, a lot is about to happen. The tidal wave of
paperwork is about to hit. There are deadlines to be met, the buyer's
inspection to navigate, and one last round of possible negotiations to
consider after the inspection. For the inexperienced, this process is
like walking through a field of land mines. And every mine you inad-
vertently step on can cost you some big bucks. This chapter is going
teach you how to avoid those mines. And you are going to learn how
to trim thousands of extra dollars out of the process.

What Is Closing?

What exactly is closing? Or as it's also known: escrow, settlement,
or under contract. By definition the closing process is "a deposit of
funds, a deed, or other instrument by one party for the delivery to
another party upon completion of a particular condition or event. It
assures that no funds or property will change hands until all of the
instructions in the transition have been followed." Now, *in English,
please!* This means that someone is selling, someone is buying. Closing, escrow, or settlement makes sure the exchange of monies and
paperwork is done properly.

After you and the seller have come to an agreement on price and terms and have signed either a purchase agreement or a contract agreement—or any of the other forms, depending on your state—you need to open escrow or notify a real estate attorney that a sale and closing need to take place within the stipulated time.

Who Are the Players?

I have to be honest with you. I think this topic is always very confusing, especially if you are moving from one state to another. I bought my first couple of houses in New Jersey, and I thought I had this whole real estate closing thing figured out. But then I moved to California, where I was completely confused by all the new players involved. The confusion happens because the name of the entity that facilitates this transfer and the process change from state to state.

The specific people and agencies that are going to be involved will vary across state lines. Even what the actual closing is called changes from state to state. For example, in California you enter into what is called escrow. However, in New York you would be "going under contract." No matter what it's labeled in your area, it means the same thing. There seems to be a general divide between East Coast and West Coast practices. But there is no clear dividing line.

East Coast Players

Okay, you say, I thought the lawyer and the real estate agent handle the deal. Well, if you are in Trenton, New Jersey, that's true. In New Jersey and New York, lawyers and real estate agents handle all the paperwork, as well as the exchange of the funds and title. In these cases, once an offer has been accepted and your deposit has been handed over, the property is considered to be "under contract" rather than "in escrow." The closing, sometimes called the settlement, then takes place on a specified date and time during which all parties meet. A settlement agent or lawyer supervises this meeting whereby the funds are disbursed per the settlement statement and the property is handed from the seller to the buyer. The deed is recorded.

West Coast Players

Most West Coast states have escrow companies that handle all the paperwork transfer and distribute all the funds. The West Coast is where escrow companies affiliated with or owned by title companies and independent escrow companies often manage the closing without needing lawyers. Escrow ensures an orderly transaction or, if something goes wrong, an orderly termination of the agreement. The seller can then give up ownership of the property, and the buyer can hand over the payment, without both parties having to be present at the same time.

Who Closes the Deal for You in Your State?

As I have said, figuring out who the players will be is half the challenge. The information that follows is based on *common* customs and practices in each state, which may not be observed in *every* closing situation. Fortunately, your Realtor will advise you on specifics as well.

According to Tony Farwell, CEO of Closing.com, their site is a great resource for homebuyers to gather more information as well as shop and compare for closing services specific to your area. Their chart below gives a rough state-by-state guide to who's involved.

Alabama	In most of the state, lawyers customarily conduct closings. In Mobile and Baldwin counties, corporate title agents may also perform closings.
Alaska	Title or escrow companies customarily conduct closings, but independent escrow agents, lenders, and lawyers may also oversee the closing.
Arizona	Title or escrow companies customarily conduct closings.
Arkansas	Title or escrow companies customarily conduct closings, but attorneys may also close the transaction.
California	In Northern California, title companies typically handle closings (through their escrow departments). In Southern California, closings are more commonly performed by dedicated escrow companies and lenders.
Colorado	Title or escrow companies customarily conduct closings, but brokers and attorneys may also close the transaction.

Connecticut	Attorneys customarily conduct closings.*
Delaware	Attorneys customarily conduct closings.*
District of Columbia	Title or abstract companies customarily conduct closings, but settlement companies and approved attorneys† may also close the transaction.
Florida	Title or escrow companies and attorneys customarily conduct closings, but they may also be handled by independent title agents.
Georgia	Attorneys customarily conduct closings.*
Hawaii	Title or escrow companies almost always conduct closings.
Idaho	Title or escrow companies usually conduct closings.
Illinois	Title or escrow companies customarily conduct closings, but lenders and attorneys may also close the transaction.
Indiana	Title or escrow companies customarily conduct closings, but lenders, real estate agents, and attorneys may also close the transaction.
Iowa	Attorneys customarily conduct closings, but they may also be performed by the title companies and real estate agents.
Kansas	Title or escrow companies customarily conduct closings, but lenders, real estate agents, and attorneys may also close the transaction.
Kentucky	Attorneys customarily conduct closings, but mortgage companies and other non-attorney entities may also close the transaction.
Louisiana	Notaries public customarily conduct closings, but attorneys and corporate title agents may also close the transaction.
Maine	Attorneys customarily conduct closings.*
Maryland	Title or escrow companies customarily conduct closings, but approved attorneys† may also close the transaction.
Massachusetts	Attorneys customarily conduct closings.†
Michigan	Title or escrow companies customarily conduct closings but lenders, real estate agents, and attorneys may also close the transaction.
Minnesota	Attorneys customarily conduct closings, but title or escrow companies, lenders, and real estate agents may also close the transaction.

Mississippi	Attorneys customarily conduct closings, but lenders may also close the transaction.
Missouri	Title or escrow companies customarily conduct closings but individual escrow agents and attorneys may also close the transaction.
Montana	Title or escrow companies customarily conduct closings, but lenders, real estate agents, and attorneys may also close the transaction.
Nebraska	Title or escrow companies customarily conduct closings, but independent title agents, brokers, and attorneys may also close the transaction.
Nevada	Title or escrow companies customarily conduct closings.
New Hampshire	Title companies and attorneys customarily conduct closings.
New Jersey	In northern New Jersey, attorneys customarily conduct closings. In southern New Jersey (below Mercer County), closings are more commonly handled by title or escrow companies.
New Mexico	Title or escrow companies customarily conduct closings.
New York	Attorneys usually conduct closings.*
North Carolina	Attorneys customarily conduct closings, but lenders may also close the transaction.
North Dakota	Title or escrow companies customarily conduct closings, but lenders, attorneys, and real estate agents may also close the transaction.
Ohio	Title or escrow companies customarily conduct closings, but lenders, attorneys, and real estate agents may also close the transaction.
Oklahoma	Title or escrow companies customarily conduct closings, but lenders, attorneys, and real estate agents may also close the transaction.
Oregon	Title or escrow companies customarily conduct closings.
Pennsylvania	Title or escrow companies customarily conduct closings, but real estate agents and approved attorneys† may also close the transaction.
Rhode Island	Attorneys and title companies customarily conduct closings, but lenders may also close the transaction.
South Carolina	Attorneys customarily conduct closings.*

South Dakota	Title or escrow companies customarily conduct closings, but lenders, real estate agents, and attorneys may also close the transaction.
Tennessee	Attorneys and title or escrow companies customarily conduct closings.
Texas	Title companies and approved attorneys[†] customarily conduct closings.
Utah	Title or escrow companies customarily conduct closings, but lenders and attorneys may also close the transaction.
Vermont	Attorneys customarily conduct closings.*
Virginia	Attorneys and title or escrow companies customarily conduct closings.
Washington	Limited Practice Officers (LPOs)[‡] and attorneys customarily conduct closings, but title or escrow companies and lenders may also close the transaction.
West Virginia	Attorneys customarily conduct closings, but occasionally lenders and real estate agents also handle the closing.
Wisconsin	Title or escrow companies customarily conduct closings, but lenders, real estate agents, and attorneys also close the transaction. In Milwaukee County, attorneys typically handle closings.
Wyoming	Title or escrow companies and attorneys customarily conduct closings, but lenders and real estate agents may also close the transaction.

Source: Closing.com, http://closingtalk.closing.com/community/learning-zone/article/who-handles-closing, accessed November 13, 2010.

* In certain states where attorneys most often conduct closings, this practice arises from the fact that real estate conveyancing has been deemed to constitute the practice of law. There is, however, a developing legal precedent in many of these states that some portion of the closing process may not constitute the "conveyancing" of real estate, and thus need not be performed by an attorney. As such, settlement companies are increasingly offering closing services in these states in which only a portion of the closing process (sometimes just the signing of transfer documents) is actually performed or supervised by an attorney.

† An "approved attorney" is one whose opinion is acceptable to a title company as the basis for issuance of a title insurance policy by the insurer.

‡ An LPO is a person certified by the Washington Supreme Court as a closing officer under rule 12 of the Admission to Practice Rules (APR).

Working with a Lawyer for Your Closing

As you see from the chart above, in certain states, you will need to have a lawyer on your team. If your state is one that requires the use of a lawyer, the most important thing is to make certain it is a real estate lawyer. You need to make sure that you are working with an attorney who does closings on a regular basis. There are so many examples of deals gone sour when people enlist a family friend or relative who is not trained in real estate and up-to-date on today's newer restrictions and guidelines. You may love Uncle Tony, who was a trial lawyer in his day, and he would do this closing for you for free, but graciously tell him thank you but no thank you.

 BYB Tip: Don't Double Your Attorney

Just as I suggest that you work with your own agent and not the listing agent when putting together your real estate deal, the same holds true for attorneys. Do not select the same attorney as your seller. In fact, try to avoid using an attorney from the same law firm. There is too much potential for conflict of interest.

The Attorney Review

In the states where attorneys are handling the closing, once you have an accepted offer, the attorney review begins. The offer is sent to both your attorney and your seller's attorney. They will each rewrite and formalize certain sections and review all the contingencies and clauses of the agreement. You will want to ask your attorney for a timeline for this review. The seller can accept a better offer if it comes along until the attorney review is complete, so you want to goose him along.

The Closing Three-Ring Circus

The closing process is truly a three-ring circus. There's something equally important going on in three different arenas—yet they all relate. Avoiding costly oversights is a real challenge for any homebuyer.

But when you know what to look for and how to stay on top of it, you can save yourself a lot of money and look forward to a successful and stress-free transaction.

Think of yourself as the ringmaster and a highly skilled juggler, jumping back and forth between the three rings. Your job is to keep all the balls in the air in each ring all at the same time! When it goes smoothly, everything comes together at closing for the big finale—making the sale happen!

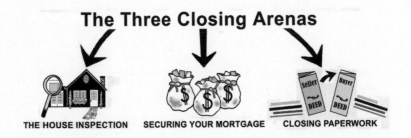

The Three Closing Arenas

THE HOUSE INSPECTION   SECURING YOUR MORTGAGE   CLOSING PAPERWORK

Closing Timeline

The key to mastering this circus is timing! With so many things happening at once and in three different arenas, without a timeline of events it's next to impossible to stay on track. That's why I like to put together a calendar of target tasks and dates—it helps create order out of chaos. Having a big-picture timeline is very helpful when setting your closing task priorities. As we review each closing task, refer back to this calendar to see just where in the timeline it falls.

Timelines can vary region by region. If attorneys handle the closings in your state, it could take considerably longer to close a sale—sixty to ninety days or so—especially if there are several attorneys involved. In states where title companies handle the closings, the turnaround time could be shorter—thirty days. If you're working with a good real estate agent, it's also his or her job to help keep the process moving as quickly as possible.

Thirty-Day Purchase Closing Timeline

May

Mon	Tues	Wed	Thurs	Fri	Sat / Sun
1 PURCHASE AGREEMENTS SIGNED	2 ESCROW OPENS! SEND IN DEPOSIT	3 BEGIN MORTGAGE PROCESS SCHEDULE INSPECTION	4	5	6/7
8 REVIEW DISCLOSURES, PLOT MAP, PERMITS	9 INSPECTION MEET WITH CONTRACTORS, TRADESMEN	10 REQUEST ESTIMATED CLOSING COSTS #1	11 NEGOTIATE INSPECTION FINDINGS	12	13/14
15	16 APPROVE TITLE REPORT	17	18	19 MORTGAGE APPROVAL DUE	20/21
22	23 REQUEST ESTIMATED CLOSING COSTS #2	24	25 SELLER TO COMPLETE REPAIRS	26 HOMEOWNERS INSURANCE SECURED	27/28
29 REQUEST ESTIMATED CLOSING COSTS #3	30 TRANSFER DOWN PAYMENT INTO ESCROW	31 FINAL WALK-THROUGH OF PROPERTY	CLOSING DAY! CONGRATULATIONS		

Your Buyer's Closing Checklist

- ❏ Submit your deposit
- ❏ The attorney review—if applicable in your state
- ❏ Schedule inspection
- ❏ Begin your mortgage search
- ❏ Review the disclosures and permits
- ❏ Complete your inspection and negotiate any concessions from the seller
- ❏ Request and review estimated closing costs statements— first pass
- ❏ Review and approve the title report
- ❏ Secure your mortgage
- ❏ Request estimated closing costs—second pass

❏ Select and secure property insurance
❏ Seller to complete termite and other requested repairs
❏ Prepare and transfer your funds to escrow
❏ Final walk-through
❏ Sign the final closing documents

One Step at a Time

You have a lot to do. And a lot to keep track of. That's why I created the sample timeline calendar above and this Buyer's Closing Checklist. This may look like an impossibly long list. But it's not. It may look scary and insurmountable. But it's not. It is a very logical step-by-step process that you can master.

The next three chapters will cover every item on this list. If you want to keep your closing on track, keep things moving smoothly, and, most important, cost effectively, you need to follow this checklist and make sure you hit every item on time. Missing a deadline is costly. And staying on top of it all will save you not only money and time— but your sanity as well!

Getting Great Closing Service

As soon as you have opened escrow, or designated a settlement office, ask for the escrow company's phone number and give them a call. Request to speak to the person who has been assigned as your escrow officer or settlement agent. It's important for you to establish a positive relationship with this person right away. Introduce yourself and say that you are looking forward to working together. Provide your cell phone number and say that you're available anytime you are needed. What you're really doing is forcing the officer to see you as an important person and not merely a case number.

Okay, okay . . . in other words, it's what we in the entertainment industry call schmoozing. You're going to want attention from this officer throughout the process. You're going to want him or her to stay on top of your closing paperwork and deadlines and to push your seller to be ready with all of his or her paperwork and obligations.

Keep in mind that by the time your officer issues you the second of your estimated closing statements, you're going to be hitting him or her up for some big-time fee reductions and junk fee removals. Having established a relationship ahead of time is going to save you some big bucks at closing.

 BYB Tip: Don't Be Afraid of Change!

If after several days and several attempts, you're unable to get your assigned escrow officer or settlement agent on the phone to introduce yourself, very politely ask for the head of the company. Tell him or her that it's important for you to be able to reach your point person occasionally, and you would like to be transferred to one who may not currently be so overwhelmed. This will either bring you to the attention of your assigned officer or get you one who will be more attentive. Remember, though, you are going to be asking for some money-saving favors later, so don't burn any bridges now.

Keeping Both You and Your Seller on Schedule

While you are juggling all the balls in the air and jumping from ring to ring, your seller can't just sit back and watch. You have a lot of deadlines to hit, but so does he. He has some responsibilities and some deadlines of his own.

Keeping your seller on track and on time is ultimately your real estate agent's responsibility. However, one of the best pieces of advice I can give you in the closing process is this: Make it your business to team up with your Realtor and stay on top of your seller's obligations as well. Find out from your Realtor, your closing officer, or your lawyer exactly what the seller's deadlines are for delivering the disclosures, ordering a termite report, making repairs, or providing any other documentation that has been negotiated.

What You Learned in This Chapter

♦ What it's called and exactly who is involved in the sale process varies from state to state.

♦ Don't feel intimidated by the volume of paperwork and plethora of people who come into play for the closing. Make sure you find out who the players are in your area.

♦ The closing process is like a three-ring circus—you are going to have to be the ringmaster and keep track of three things going on all at once.

♦ Not only are you responsible for your own obligations and deadlines, but you need to keep track of your seller's deadlines and the closing company's paperwork as well.

♦ Despite the apparent chaos to the closing, it's a methodical step-by-step process that you can master if you team up with your Realtor and/or your lawyer and stay involved.

CHAPTER 13

The House Inspection

The house inspection is one of your most powerful buying tools. With the flood of foreclosed, abandoned, and distressed properties that have hit the market, it's imperative to know exactly what this house is all about both inside and out before you run to the closing table to sign on the dotted line.

Having the property inspected before closing serves as a critical step in the home-buying process. The home inspection ensures that any problems are discovered long before you finalize the deal, guarantees the worthiness of your financial investment, and decreases the possibility of purchasing a property with major structural or other serious problems that will lead to significant unforeseen costs for you.

It's an essential part of the process that protects you in three different but equally invaluable ways.

Three Ways the Home Inspection Protects You

1. **Know Your House from Top to Bottom**—This is your chance to bring in a knowledgeable professional inspector who will fully inspect and analyze the property inside and out. The inspector goes over every system from plumbing to electrical, every crawl space, and every door and window to find all the defects

you couldn't possibly have identified on your own while house hunting.

2. **Have a Way Out**—The inspection contingency in your purchase agreement gives you time to consider and reconsider your purchase. It buys you an extra seven to ten days to decide if this property is all that you hoped it would be. If for any reason you find something physically wrong with the house during the inspection that does not feel manageable or fixable to you, you can walk away from the deal—without penalty.

3. **Renegotiate Your Deal**—Inspection allows you to continue to negotiate. Within three to five days afterward, you may request that the sellers fix any problems discovered, from the serious to the simple; give you a cash credit toward the cost of the repairs or toward closing costs; or reduce the price of the property to reflect the repair costs. If they refuse, you can walk away and take your deposit with you.

Hiring the Inspector

Finding your inspector is not that difficult. You can generally get the best inspector referrals from your real estate agent, family, friends, neighbors, or anyone who has recently purchased a home in your same area.

Here are the qualities you want:

- **He is licensed.** Not all states require this. But try to find one that is a member of the American Society of Home Inspectors (ASHI) at www.ashi.com.

- **He lets you tag along with him during the inspection.**

- **He is tough.** You want someone who is meticulous and points out every little problem. It is to your advantage to have a long list after he's finished.

- **He has a working knowledge of renovations.** Find out ahead of time if you will be able to ask him repair questions as the inspection is in progress.

- **He writes up the report on the spot.** That's what laptops are for. Get a copy from him ASAP.

- **His fee is reasonable.** Your real estate agent will know what's standard in your locale. The average inspection costs $300 to $500, including the written report.

Seller's Disclosures—Demand Them before Inspection Day

Simply put, the seller's disclosures are the written statements that disclose, inform, and reveal any and all problems or issues that a home seller knows about his or her house.

As we discussed in an earlier chapter, you will want to have as much information about your prospective new home as you can. But now that you are about to have your inspection, you are absolutely entitled, and in most states legally entitled, to have a copy of the seller's disclosure statements. I always ask for this document to be presented upon acceptance of my offer. That gives me a week to review it prior to the inspection. I know what additional problems, if any, there will be to address. If the seller discloses a serious roof leak, I'll know ahead of time to bring a roofer to the inspection for an estimate.

Nine Disclosures to Demand Prior to Inspection

1. Seller's Disclosure Statement

What exactly is the seller obligated to disclose? Good question. By law in Oklahoma, for instance, a defect that must be disclosed is defined as any "condition, malfunction, or problem that would have a materially adverse effect on the monetary value of the property, or that would impair the health or safety of future occupants of the property." Even if you're not selling a home in Oklahoma, this definition is a good one to remember.

The seller's disclosure statement is usually a two- to five-page preprinted form with lots of yes/no questions that itemize all the possible areas of the home that may be in need of repair or are defective. The seller is obligated to include all known problems, outstanding permit issues, any problems with neighbors, or even the fact that a serious crime has been committed in the home. It also includes environmental problems such as the presence of radon or lead paint.

Your Realtor can tell you what types of disclosures sellers are obliged to make in your area. Obviously, different regions of the country will require different focal points on disclosures. For example, you can expect to find questions about flooding in South Carolina, whereas in California, you can expect questions about earthquake damage.

The disclosure offers no warranty. It is only a statement of facts as known by the seller. But without it, a seller and his Realtor may be liable when and if preexisting problems pop up once you have bought the house.

2. Copies of All Previous Inspections

Request copies of any previous inspections. If there have been other buyers before you that have performed inspections, then their discoveries are a huge wealth of information for you. Ask for the copies of these reports right away.

3. Copies of All Permits

Ask for a presentation of all permits on the property so you'll know more about what you're looking at—and for—during inspection. Some sellers' Realtors don't like to do this, while others will happily comply. If your seller won't do so, get the permits yourself. Your Realtor will advise you on how to obtain them. You want to know if that room addition was done with a permit or if the new copper plumbing was installed by a professional or a handyman.

The consequence of not checking out the permits can be expensive. If you decide to buy the house and later perform renovations, you'll need to apply for a permit. If there is a history of which you are not aware—such as an unapproved permit that has been floating around since an old room addition—you'll have to pay to bring it up to code. If it wasn't done right in the first place, you'll have to redo the original job. Or someday when you decide to sell, you'd have to disclose that these items were never permitted, and that could be a problem for your future buyer as well. The only way to be sure is to see the permits yourself now.

4. Copy of the Plat Map

This is a map that clearly defines your property lines and the size of your land lot. Yes, I know most people call it the plot map, but it is actually the plat map. Once you have the plat map, if there is still a question, you may need to do a site survey. You would be surprised how many times the property lines are not exactly where the sellers think they are. A confirmation of the actual lot lines can go either way. I have discovered extra land—a big boon when I went to sell. Another time I was very disappointed because a big section of the property was on a city easement and I was unable to develop the backyard.

5. Copy of the CC&Rs

"CC&Rs" stands for covenants, conditions, and restrictions. Each is a set of rules that specifies what you can and can't do with your home or condo. This is invaluable information to have prior to your inspection, in the event you discover issues that might need repair or attention yet are restricted by the CC&Rs.

Developers create CC&Rs to establish rules when they create a subdivision and want to control what buyers will do with their houses. You may be restricted to the exterior colors you can use on the house, the style of windows you can install, or the kind of trees you can plant. Restrictions can also be placed on condos, co-ops, planned unit developments, and any subdivision that's governed by a homeowners association.

6. Copies of Historic Preservation Overlay Zone Bylaws

"HPOZ" stands for Historic Preservation Overlay Zone. It may not be called exactly this in your state, but it refers to any district, neighborhood, block, or even building that has been designated historical. HPOZs are actually very beneficial and a plus for you as a buyer because they guarantee that your neighbors will have to adhere to a strict code of design review standards. A homeowner will never have to worry that the house next door will be torn down and replaced by a behemoth McMansion. But then again, before you can make any changes to an HPOZ-designated home, you'll have to go before the review board.

7. Property Taxes

Get a copy of the current tax bill. It's important to review so there are no surprises.

8. Utilities

Not a bad idea to ask for a copy of the seller's utility bills. It's helpful for you to determine the age and efficiency of the current systems.

9. Copies of Receipts or Warranty Info for Any Major Improvements

This includes documentation for major renovations to roofs, heating and air, etc.

Let the Inspection Begin

I think inspection day is exciting. It's an opportunity to spend an extended period of time in your new prospective house. Plus you get to explore every nook and cranny, every closet and attic. You get to turn on all the faucets and run the showers. You get to test all the appliances, even peel back a corner of the wall-to-wall carpet to see if there is hardwood underneath. But most important, you have the opportunity find out everything there is to know about the workings of this house translated through an expert's eyes.

Bring Your Problems with You

By this point in the home buying if you've learned anything from what I've talked about so far you will most likely have used the Fix-It Hit List in chapter 6 to begin to identify noticeable problems or items that need attention in the house. Bring it with you on inspection day. Also have all the seller's disclosures and previous inspections, if there were any, with you to present to the inspector. You're going to want to make sure that the inspector identifies all of the issues and discusses each and every one with you.

Inspect with the Inspector

A good house inspection can take up to three hours, or longer. So bring a coffee and a good book, right? Wrong—really wrong! A major key to home-buying success is to inspect with the inspector.

 BYB Tip: Always Dog the Inspector

Always follow the inspector as he works his way through the house. Don't sit around and gab with the Realtor. Follow the inspector around like an annoying puppy dog. Watch and ask questions. His knowledge is invaluable. Don't miss this opportunity.

I tag along with my notebook in hand and say things like, "Oh, really . . . how much might this cost to repair? Is it major? Is that really serious or is it fixable?" Believe me, this is the best crash course in home fix-its and renovations you can get!

Take notes and jot down things he says as he works through the inspection. Once he puts it in the report, it becomes set in stone and subject to legal problems if something is contested. So he'll tend to soft-pedal when he puts it in writing. In person, he'll often give you the worst-case scenario and some extra info and advice.

What to Inspect

What to inspect? Everything. It's important to examine all areas of the home, including the exterior, interior, attic, basement, electric, plumbing, and heating and air systems. Faulty construction, improper electrical wiring, inefficient insulation, old heating, building permit violations, and other unseen problems can lead to expensive home repairs large and small. You and your inspector need to examine every square inch of the house—from the electric garage door to the built-in microwave. While every component of the house is equally important and can bring forth an opportunity to renegotiate, there are some areas that I like to call the inspection hot spots.

Inspection Hot Spots

- Electrical

- Plumbing

- Heating and air

- Roof

- Foundation

- Attics

- Drainage

- Nonconforming use

Electrical

Check the electrical panel. If an older home has modern circuit breakers instead of the age-appropriate fuse box, it has been upgraded. You may still have to add in more capacity, but that is much less costly. Most upgraded houses of around 2,000 square feet need approximately 200 amps. A really big house (3,500 to 5,000 square feet) may need up to 400 amps.

Plumbing

Test the water. Does it get hot? How long does it take? What is the water pressure like if more than one sink is running? Turn on several faucets and flush a toilet or two at the same time. If the water pressure drops, plan to do some work on the piping. Is the piping plastic, copper, galvanized, or lead? Does the house have a basement with easy pipe access or is it built on a clement slab? If it's a slab, factor in increased costs for big plumbing repairs. Make sure the piping is consistent throughout. Whenever possible I like to replace the plumbing with new copper piping, using companies that specialize in full replumbing and can do the entire house in a matter of days. After your inspection you will know exactly what the plumbing issues are.

Water heaters should always be new, or nearly new. Use a flashlight to look for any rust on the bottom. Ask your inspector if they are vented and placed properly according to code. Also confirm that they are of adequate capacity.

Heating and Air

How old is the system? Any rooms missing vents or ducts? If the systems are eight years of age or older, they may be a problem about to happen, or something you may want to replace soon after you buy. Most important, does it cool the entire house? Does it heat the entire house properly? No matter the weather at the time of inspection—sweltering or frigid—check both the heating and the air.

Roof

Ask your inspector if he is certified to inspect the roof. This is a good question to ask when you first hire the inspector. Some inspectors are not and you will need to call in a roof specialist to climb up there.

Foundation

This may be your only opportunity to peer under the house. Use it. What kind of foundation are you dealing with? Is it wood footings with a cement base, a stone foundation with a basement, a cement

BYB Tip: Wintertime Inspections

Keep in mind that if you are doing an inspection in snowy weather, it may be very difficult to access and examine the roof. Realtors in the northern states are familiar with this problem. It may be possible to have a special provision that allows you to extend the inspection contingency specifically to accommodate the roof, in the hopes that the weather improves.

slab, or a raised foundation with a crawl space? Each one has pros and cons.

There are regional tendencies. The East Coast and Northeast tend to have basements. Coastal areas and states like Florida and earthquake-prone states like California rarely do. Houses there are often built on cement slabs, which can be a real challenge if you want to make any plumbing changes to move sinks, toilets, showers, or gas-burning appliances. Factor in those costs.

Visible Foundation Defects

Look for cracks in the walls, particularly around fireplaces or in foundation walls. Uneven floors and tilted stairways could indicate there has been movement in the foundation. Also, notice doors that are not perfectly vertical. If there is more space between a door and its frame at one end than at the other, the door is likely installed incorrectly.

Attics

Check the insulation. Look for signs of roof leaks. Examine any visible heating and air ducts. By the way, while you are up there determine if you can convert the attic—might be something to think about down the line.

Drainage

Sure, it may be the middle of summer and it's a beautiful sunny day out. And it hasn't rained in weeks, maybe even months. But every neighborhood, even in the driest parts of the country, will go through its rainy season. And you need to know what happens when it does.

Ask your inspector to take a look at the exterior drainage issues. When it rains will water from the roof flow away from the house toward the street or will it drain into your basement or rot out your foundation?

Are you on a riverbank? Or near a river, lake, or pond? If so, talk to your neighbors to find out if in the worst conditions that pond has ever overflowed and submerged your backyard.

My Rainy Day Flooding Story

In my hometown of Collingswood, New Jersey, once every couple of years we would be inundated with a monsoonlike rainstorm. We lived a block away from the Cooper River. And like clockwork every time those monsoon rains hit, the Cooper River would overflow and flood out at least two or three of our neighbors. Fortunately our house was built on high enough ground that we were never overrun by the floodwater. And even though it was a tragic time for my neighbors, at eight years old I still loved to jump in my dad's rowboat and paddle around the neighborhood.

The point of this story is talk to the neighbors and find out what happens during those rainy seasons every few years when the lake banks swell and the neighborhood kids trade in their bikes for boats.

Nonconforming Use

Converted garages, sun porches, or add-on bedrooms can increase square footage, but when done without permits, they can also add headaches when it's time to make them legal. You may be better off

---

 BYB Tip: Come Out with a Closet

In order to be legally considered a bedroom, there must be a closet in the room. So your advertised three-bedroom may really only be a two-bedroom and a den. This can come back to bite you when you go to sell someday.

ripping them down rather than bearing the cost of permitting something you didn't build before sale. It may not be worth the expense. Having the house permits with you when you inspect will help you confirm what conforms and what doesn't.

Other Inspections You May Need, to Cover Your . . . Assets

Don't assume that if you hire a home inspector, he will be able to tell you absolutely everything you need to know about the house. They will cover almost everything, but you might have to fill in a few blanks. Home inspectors are very careful not to take on liability for issues that are outside their area of expertise. Which means the overall basic home inspection is your first step. There are additional inspections you may need to do to make sure you are totally covered.

■ **Chimney Inspection**—Your regular inspector may not do this, but if there is any question of stability or structural damage, have a chimney specialist do a "chimney cam" and run a small video camera down the chimney to see it from the inside.

■ **Geological Inspection**—Especially for hillside and cliffside properties, or in flood areas, a geological inspection can unearth a severe drainage or ground-shifting problem—and save you thousands from further damage.

■ **Sewer Inspection**—A sewer expert can use a "sewer cam" to discover cracks or breaks in the sewer line from the house to the street—especially on properties that are heavily landscaped, where root growth can crack and clog the pipeline. This can be a serious expense, so find out now.

■ **Termite Inspection**—This is usually done by the seller because most mortgage companies and banks will need it prior to allowing a loan on the house. But whoever does it, make sure you review the finished report and all the recommended work is taken care of.

■ **Moisture, Mold, and Toxins Inspection**—Honestly I think this mold inspection thing has been blown up a bit—more hype than reality. However, it's important to check for moisture in any basement or below-ground-level areas. Moisture is an indicator of the potential for a mold problem—if there isn't one already.

Check for asbestos if the house was built prior to 1975. You may find it on insulation around ducting, water heaters, and pipes. If it is accessible and can be removed by an asbestos specialist, then maybe this is something you might want to ask the seller to do.

 BYB Tip: Are They Hiding Something?

The nose knows. On the day of inspection, are the windows wide open, and one or two of the doors, even if it's freezing outside? Well, that sounds like a red flag to me. Or has someone recently sprayed air freshener or been burning scented candles? If so, it smells to me like the seller has something nasty to cover up. So keep your nose at the ready at all times, especially when inspecting the basement, attic, and crawl spaces.

Preconstruction, Under Construction, and New Construction—Inspect along the Way

Just because you're buying a spanking new home that is in the process of being built doesn't mean you can bypass the inspection process. It's a good idea to get an expert eye on a new home as it is being built. And if you can, have someone check out the house-in-progress. Get someone who can identify mediocre work or potential problems. You can oftentimes hire an inspector or an outside contractor to stop by the property and then pay him an hourly rate. It is money well invested. The following five stages are of particular interest:

1. Once the foundation is poured

2. Once the framing is complete

3. Once the plumbing and wiring are installed

4. Just prior to finishes and painting

5. After completion prior to closing

> ⚠ **BYB Buyer's Blunder: Skipping a Full Inspection on a New Property**
>
> Learn from my mistake. Several years ago, I purchased a home in Palm Springs, California, that was brand new and had been completed recently by a local builder. I had the inspector come to do the basic inspection. At the time I thought that since it was new construction, I probably could forgo having some of the additional inspections and maybe save a little money. So I never bothered to have a sewer line inspection.
>
> About a month after being in the home and having friends stay for several weekends visiting from out of town, every sink, toilet, tub, and shower began to back up. Try as we might to unclog the drains, we could not, and the smell began to grow worse and worse. In desperation I called a sewer line specialist to come out for an emergency visit.
>
> As it turned out, a balloon-type mechanism that the builder and plumber had used to install the sewer line had never been removed from the sewer line. Everything that should have been draining out of the house had been backed up underneath the house for three weeks. It took four days with all the doors and windows open to get the house back to its "new house" smell. Had I done my sewer inspection at the time of my purchase I would've saved myself from a lot of aggravation and a stinky few weeks.

How to Negotiate after the Inspection

Your inspection report will most likely be full of problems and repairs large and small. Just expect that and don't panic. It's the inspector's job to find everything that is wrong. If it's an older home, one that has been in foreclosure, or simply one whose owners have deferred maintenance, that list may get really long. And many times, new construction has just as many issues, from unfinished details to shoddy construction.

Thus, between the inspection report and the seller's disclosure statement, you will have a handful of repairs and problems ranging from minor to serious. But you are now about to put these problems on the negotiating table with the seller.

Getting a Better Deal

So you thought the negotiation process was over. Nope, you have another round. But this is a good thing; it legitimately gives you the opportunity to see if things can be resolved with repairs, replacement, credit, or a drop in price. It's time to open negotiations all over again now that the inspection report is in. Thanks to your inspection contingency, you can walk away from the deal without penalty if any issues are revealed in either the seller's disclosure or the inspection report that you don't like.

But don't walk just yet. Let's negotiate a better deal instead.

During the contractual time period, usually within five days after inspection, have your real estate agent submit a list of the repairs you are requesting to be made or to be credited for their value. For example, if the hot water heater is rusted out and ready to keel over, you can ask to have it replaced or get a credit for the $650 repair cost. Or, better yet, ask for a price reduction on the house.

Bigger problems create bigger negotiating opportunities. If you're potentially dealing with roof issues, a crumbly foundation, or sketchy heating and air, you will immediately bring in a professional—a contractor or structural engineer—to assess the situation, advise you on what steps to take, and estimate how much it will cost to bring the house up to speed.

Let's say the inspection report indicates that the roof is on its last gasp and already leaking. Quick, get a roofer out there to give you an idea of what the new roof will cost. Get an estimate written up. Ask your sellers for the $6,000 repair credit. The sellers are now put on notice that if they don't replace the old roof, or you are not credited the $6,000 in the purchase price, then you have the option to walk away.

The sellers of course can say no, and then your deal is off. You get your deposit back and they put the house back on the market, and you have to start house shopping all over again.

However, more often than not, the sellers will be a bit flexible and open to negotiation.

Three Reasons Why These Sellers May Agree to Fix or Credit Back

1. Once a problem is discovered, revealed, or identified in your in-spection, by law the sellers must disclose it to any other future buyers. They will *have to* deal with it. And chances are the next buyer will ask for the same credit or price reduction anyway.
2. Inspection credit negotiations usually come nearly two weeks into the escrow process. During that time your sellers are al-ready making moving plans and assuming the deal will go through. It's in their best interests to make the deal work and give some concessions, rather than start all over again.
3. Most sellers' Realtors don't want to start from scratch, find a new buyer, and put together a whole new deal. It's double work for the same commission. So the sellers' Realtor will be giving them an extra goose to come up with some concessions.

 BYB Tip: Wait Till the Last Minute

Wait until the last minute to submit your request for credits or re-pairs. The longer the property has been tied up and off the market, the more pressure on the seller to meet your demands. But let me be clear here, *do not* miss your deadline to ask for concessions. Even if your contingency period expires by a day, you will lose your legal right to negotiate the repairs.

 BYB Tip: Don't Overnegotiate the Inspection Report

Don't get *too* cocky. You might overnegotiate yourself out of a deal. And a buyer that overnegotiates is a red flag to a savvy seller's agent. If you are too difficult and demanding now in the beginning of this deal, the seller and his agent would only expect that behav-ior to continue. They may sense more of a headache ahead than a closable deal and be happy to let you walk away.

What You Learned in This Chapter

♦ A home inspection protects you in three ways. You uncover the existing problems with the house; you are legally entitled to get out of the deal if you don't like what you find; and you have an opportunity to renegotiate with the seller.

♦ Make sure you have all the seller's disclosures in hand prior to your inspection.

♦ Always inspect with your inspector. Be by his side at all times during the inspection. You'll gain a wealth of information.

♦ Make sure to inspect everything. This is your chance. And if your inspector's area of expertise does not include something like sewer lines or chimneys, hire an additional expert if need be.

♦ It's a big mistake to skip doing a full inspection on new construction.

♦ This is the time to negotiate to have your seller make needed repairs, give you credit for their cost, or lower the price of the house to reflect the expenses.

♦ Don't overnegotiate and ask for too much—you may negotiate yourself right out of a deal.

CHAPTER 14

Shopping for a Mortgage

I'll admit, I saved this chapter for last when writing this book. It's truly one of the most volatile and constantly changing topics in real estate. And it's one of the scariest topics for homebuyers today. The entire mortgage industry and how it transacts business has shifted dramatically in the past five years. Gone are the days when anyone could walk into a bank and get a big loan without proof of income, assets, or even verified ability to make the monthly payments. You can forget about picking up the phone, calling a bank or mortgage broker, and securing a no-hassle and pain-free mortgage. As we discussed in the first chapter, those lenders who handed out easy qualification and subprime loans were badly burned when the market started to turn south.

Fortunately the banking industry has been forced to reexamine how it lends money and how it does business in general. Today's new market reflects a return to the traditional conservative lending criteria and standards banks had used for decades.

These "new" standards are back and are now in place to protect both lenders and borrowers over the long term. Rightfully so, lenders have tightened their eligibility guidelines and are doling out loans only to the most creditworthy borrowers, the ones who have the cash for the down payment and the income to pay the monthly payments.

Getting a Mortgage Today—What to Expect

Some potential homebuyers believe that mortgage money is nearly impossible to secure today, a myth repeated often in the press. That doesn't mean that it's impossible to qualify for a mortgage these days, but it is much more difficult. As I just pointed out, mortgage money is available to those with proven income, solid credit history, and established employment. And it really is possible to lock in a mortgage that is safe, secure, and affordable. Yes, it's going to be more challenging and time consuming, but if you know what to expect, you'll be prepared for the securitization.

Getting a Mortgage Today—What to Expect

- Plan to put more money down and borrow less.

- There are requirements for larger down payments—20 percent for a single-family home and as much as 30 percent for a multiunit property.

- Qualifying standards are higher—more documentation, proof of income, proof of job security, et cetera.

- Finding the right mortgage requires new levels of conditions and more homework.

- The terms are not going to be as sweet.

- It will cost you more—you will probably have to pay a fee or "points."

- It will take longer—don't bank on less than forty-five-day closings.

The New Rules of Borrowing

Before we talk about the dos and don'ts of getting a mortgage, and the best and worst mortgages for today's market, I want to remind you of one of the first New Rules for Today's New Market we discussed: **Put 20 percent down.**

I talked about it at length back in chapter 2. But now in this chapter, it really comes into play. Because with all the rules and types of mortgages we will discuss, they are all building upon my advice in this rule: Put 20 Percent Down! Okay, I promise to stop harping about it now. I think I made my point.

So now let me throw one more safeguard at you. Again when it comes to buying safe, sane, and smart, you have to buy affordable as well. This next rule helps you answer the question *How much should I borrow?* It's the question people ask immediately after *How much can I afford?* I am all about teaching you to buy within your means and never overextend your financial reach, and this one embodies the safeguard you need.

New Rule: Whatever the Bank Will Lend You, Take 20 Percent Less

—David Bach, New York Times *bestselling author of*
Start Late, Finish Rich

Let's say you go to a bank or a mortgage broker to get preapproved for a mortgage. You say, "I want to buy a house; how much of a mortgage will you give me?" In other words, "What price house can I afford?" The bank or mortgage broker will evaluate your finances, income, and savings and say, "Well, Mr. Smith, we think that you can qualify for a $400,000 mortgage. Which means you can buy a house for $500,000! Congratulations."

Here's where David Bach's new rule kicks in. If they are offering you a $400,000 loan, say, "No, thanks." Subtract 20 percent from that loan amount and bank on a $320,000 loan instead. Thus the house you should really be shopping for will need to be around $400,000. By taking 20 percent less of a loan than what the bank has to offer, you are safeguarding yourself and your financial security. You automatically create a built-in buffer for yourself in case of an unforeseen problem.

I have worked many times with David Bach. In fact, we were on tour together in 2009 with the Real Estate and Wealth Expo lecturing around the country. I really like his perspective and his clear, succinct strategies. His approach to finance and money management is straightforward, logical, practical, and powerful. This new rule is not only a simple and clever concept, but it's also a fantastic way to protect yourself in any type of market.

> **In this new market—Borrow Less, Borrow Safe, Borrow Smart.**

The Best Mortgages for Today's New Market

The Traditional 30- or 15-Year Fixed Mortgage

I *always* recommend that you get a 15- or 30-year fixed mortgage—even if you are planning to stay in your new home for only a short while. You never know what may happen in your life, and you want to know that you have a safe and consistent mortgage payment every month for the life of the loan.

Once again, I am dating myself, but I am willing to suffer the label of old age if it saves you from financial ruin ten years from now. Interest rates do not always hover around 5 and 6 percent. Oh, no. It may seem unbelievable to you today, but I remember buying a property and being thrilled that I was able to lock in a fixed rate at only 12.5 percent! That's right, within the past few decades, interest rates have actually gone to over 14 percent. And that could easily happen again.

I want you to have the confidence that the mortgage payment amount you have today will be the mortgage payment amount you'll be paying ten or fifteen years from now, no matter what the market or the economy is doing.

The Next Best Mortgages for Today's New Market

The Adjustable Rate Mortgage (ARM)

There are many variations of an adjustable rate mortgage, or ARM. But the common denominator is that the interest rate and payment can change over the term of the loan. It can start low, which helps you qualify when rates are high, and then it adjusts in one, three, five, or seven years. But as we've already seen, you cannot predict how high the adjustment will go—potentially pushing you further and further away from what's affordable. Which is why these loans are not ideal.

What You Need to Know about ARMs

The interest rate on an ARM is linked to an economic index. Common indexes used by lenders include the activity of one, three, and five-year Treasury securities, but there are many others. Each ARM is linked to a specific index, which dictates changes in your rate—periodically adjusting up or down as the relevant index changes. A standard ARM will adjust and rise or fall monthly depending upon the current market rates. You may see an ARM described with figures such as 1-2, 1-1, 3-1, and 5-1. These are fixed-rate adjustable mortgages. The first figure in each set refers to the initial period of the loan, during which your interest rate will stay the same as it was on the day you signed your loan papers. The second number is the adjustment period, showing how often adjustments can be made to the rate after the initial period has ended. Thus, if you have a 5-1 loan, your payment will be the same or fixed for the first five years, but after that, it will readjust every year to the current market rate, for the life of the loan.

There are, however, caps on total interest charged on these mortgages. *Periodic* caps limit the amount your interest rate can increase from one adjustment period to the next. Not all ARMs have periodic rate caps. *Overall* caps, which have been required by law since 1987, limit how much the interest rate can increase over the life of the loan. Again translated into English: If you have an adjustable-rate loan, ask about your periodic caps and your overall lifetime cap. If a loans is currently 6 percent, then the lifetime cap could be 10 percent and your interest rate can never go higher. But a word of caution here. If you are used to a payment at 5 percent, and it jumps to 10 percent, you could quickly be in deep trouble.

FHA Loans

As discussed in chapter 2, loans backed by the Federal Housing Administration don't require large down payments, which is why they gained popularity in recent years. And also as we discussed in chapter 2, I don't suggest anyone apply for a loan with less than 20 percent down. The fact that these loans will qualify buyers with only 3.5 percent down payments really scares me. And it should scare you, too. If you can only scrape together 3.5 percent for a down payment, then I say you can't afford and should not buy a house just yet.

That said, I feel I have to at least discuss and explain FHA-backed mortgages because they currently comprise 33 to 36 percent of the market. And many mortgage brokers and banks do offer them. You'll simply need to go to an FHA-approved lender, which you can find by going to www.hud.gov and searching online using your zip code under its "lender locator" function. Contrary to what you might think, the FHA does not actually make loans or guarantee loans; it *insures* loans. The insurance removes or minimizes the risk lenders face when buyers put down less than 20 percent. That is why lenders are willing to accept less than 20 percent down from the homebuyers on these loans. Other facts about these loans that you should consider if you want to apply for one:

- You'll need a credit score of at least 640. The interest rate you will be offered will reflect your credit score. The lower your credit score, the higher your interest rate and vice versa.

- You'll only need to put down at least 3.5 percent, and hopefully you can come up with a lot more . . . please.

- FHA loans allow for higher debt-to-income levels than lenders conventionally allow. Meaning your income does not need to be as high as it would have to be on a non-FHA loan.

- You'll additionally pay mortgage insurance each month, which is at least 0.9 percent of the loan.

- You'll need to stay within certain limits with regard to purchase price. FHA-backed loans will only cover up to a certain amount based on location. The current FHA limit has been raised in some counties; in Los Angeles County, for example, the FHA limit is $729,500 (in 2010). However, in Denver, Colorado, it's only $406,250.

Mortgages to Avoid in Today's New Market

Creative Financing

In this new market, the time has passed for homebuyers to acquire properties creatively. The funky "creative" loan programs that started to become available and popular around the year 2000 are dead. Those loans were designed to make the homebuyer's initial monthly mortgage payments as small as possible and to help homebuyers qualify for their loans. But, in keeping with their sometimes name of "liar loans,"

New Rule: Avoid Teaser Rate and Balloon Payment Loans

—Mellody Hobson, president of Ariel Investments and financial contributor to ABC's Good Morning America

A great many people signed up for short-term teaser loans and mortgages that had enormous balloon payments within three to five years or adjustable rates that began to recalculate after three years. They believed that the market would always stay strong and house prices would continue to skyrocket endlessly. They never questioned their ability to refinance their ever-appreciating house with its escalating value. These house purchases of yesterday are the very same houses of today that have been forced into foreclosure.

Mellody Hobson is a brilliant financial expert, and she is adamant about this. In talking with her about creative financing, one of the first things she said to me was, "The good news is that it's nearly impossible in this new market for borrowers to get those terrible, creative—or as I call them, extreme—mortgages any longer."

those $1,200-per-month teaser rates quickly ballooned into $4,000 monthly payments—a huge contributing factor to the meltdown of the real estate market.

These creative mortgages include interest-only loans, loans with artificially low preliminary teaser rates, balloon loans, negative amortized or wraparound loans, seller financing, personal notes or loans, even borrowing on credit cards.

In this new market, creative financing literally translates to . . . foreclosure in two to three years. So don't even consider it. Stick to conventional loans with conventional lending institutions. Heed Mellody's advice and stop getting creative. Save that for your decorating—not your financing.

Interest-Only Loans

Are you insane? This is a loan that can be either fixed rate or adjustable. Either way, you only pay on the interest of the loan each month. You never pay anything toward principal. In today's market this is a terrible loan because most homeowners continue to pay only this amount and never pay off any principal. In thirty years, they will have paid hundreds of thousands of dollars in interest and still owe the original loan amount. Walk away from any of these loans, even though they can be tempting.

 BYB Tip: No Prepayment Penalties

Make sure to ask for a loan that has *no* prepayment penalties. Yes, you may be planning to own this home for many years, but things happen and timelines change. If you do have to sell sooner than expected, you don't want to be penalized for it. If you learn that there's a prepayment penalty, consider walking away or asking that it be taken out of the agreement. In some states, prepayment penalties are no longer allowed. But some lenders will try to collect an additional six months of "unearned interest" if you pay the loan off early through a refinance or sale of the property. The only prepayment penalty you can consider is what's called a "soft prepay." If you hold on to the property for over one year, you will avoid any penalty.

BYB Tip: Lock in Your Rate

When rates are on the rise, it's good to get your interest rate locked in. That way, if it goes up before you close, you get to keep your original rate. But make sure the time it's locked in for matches the length of your projected closing. If you are lucky and rates are going lower, there's no point to locking in. But if have locked in a rate and you're not sure which way the rate is going, protect yourself by asking for a "float down." This way, if rates happen to drop lower, you can float down along with it and get that interest rate.

Conforming vs. Jumbo Loans—Terms to Know

You hear these terms bandied about all the time. So here is a quick explanation. A conforming loan is defined today as any loan amounting to $417,000 or less. You can borrow up to that amount and your loan would be called "conforming." The next price limit above that is considered to be a "high balance conforming loan." The maximum limit for this loan is set by Freddie Mac and Fannie Mae, and it depends upon where you live. For example, in Los Angeles the limit for these loans is $729,000. However, in Hawaii or New York City, it's higher—around $790,000. The interest rates for high balance conforming loans will be a bit higher than for conforming loans. And higher still are the interest rates on the loans labeled jumbo loans. These are the loans whose amounts exceed the high balance loan limits.

In today's market these limits and guidelines change regularly, so make sure to ask exactly in which category you would fall.

Banks vs. Mortgage Brokers

The difference between a mortgage broker and a bank loan officer can be confusing if you've never worked with either one before. Though they both aim to get you into a house with a mortgage, they are not the same.

Mortgage Brokers

Mortgage brokers are professionals who are paid a fee to bring together lenders and borrowers. They usually have access to dozens of different lenders. It helps to think of mortgage brokers as agents. They will evaluate your credit situation to determine which lender is the best fit for your needs. The broker submits your application to one or more lenders in order to sell it, and she works with the chosen lender until the loan closes. Brokers specialize in customizing the mortgage to your unique needs. They can often find a lender who will make loans to people that a bank refuses, such as those with problem credit.

They make their money by getting 1 to 1.5 percent of the mortgage, and their fee is paid by the lender. Thus, it does not necessarily cost you more, as brokers often work with the wholesale departments at banks, which allows you to end up paying the same with a reputable mortgage broker as you would dealing directly with the bank. Besides a great rate, your mortgage broker can get you that preapproval letter we covered in chapter 4, which turbocharges you into a dream buyer.

How to Find a Mortgage Broker

As with your Realtor, the best way to find a mortgage broker is through references. Talk to your friends. If you've found your Realtor,

 BYB Tip: Get It Up Front

Stephen Gandel, senior writer at *Time* magazine, suggests that, when shopping for a mortgage broker, try to find brokers who will disclose their commissions from the lenders up front. They are actually called "up-front mortgage brokers." The advantage is that they disclose the set fee or commission that they will be receiving from the bank or lender. It then allows them to suggest all available mortgage options to you fairly, without being influenced by banks that are offering to pay higher commissions to put you into a loan that may not necessarily be in your best interests. He suggests going to www.upfrontmortgagebrokers.org to get a list of those mortgage brokers in your area.

ask him or her. In fact, while you're interviewing your Realtors, ask them who they've worked with and respected.

What to Look for—and Expect

When you get the mortgage broker on the phone, which should be easy—or move on to the next—ask for the names of banks and lenders with whom she has relationships. Find out how long she has been doing this. Ask if she is specially trained and licensed. You want someone with at least five years of experience.

Banks

Banks offer an opportunity to work directly with the entity that will be offering you the loan. Loan officers at banks or credit unions are employees who work to sell and process mortgages and other loans *originated by their employer.* They often have a wide variety of loan types to draw from, but all loans originate from their one bank. So a loan officer at Wells Fargo, for instance, will sell mortgages created by Wells Fargo. He won't be offering you a loan from Citibank or SunBank. The loan officer takes your application and works to find a home loan that suits your needs.

Walk into your local bank and speak face-to-face with its loan officer. Using a local bank can sometimes be a plus. The staff generally understands the specifics of local properties, whereas a distant lender, including online banks, may not. And there's still something to be said for making personal contact when trying to convince someone to lend you money in today's market. If your personal credit is approved, the officer moves forward to process the purchase. Though a loan officer may not get a fee out of the deal like a mortgage broker will, there are likely to be other fees related to the transaction that enrich the bank for closing your deal.

Shop Around for a Loan

Don't expect to find the best loan the first time you speak to either a broker or a bank. It pays to shop around and engage both brokers and banks in search of ideal loan terms. You don't have to sign an exclusivity agreement with anyone when you're looking to land a mortgage, but you can certainly let those you speak to know that you're shopping around and applying for more than one loan. You never know who will say yes first or charge the least amount of fees or points. You want to gather as many options as possible and see which numbers make the most sense to you—and which lender will come through for you and your needs.

The difference between accepting a bank's mortgage program directly or working with a broker could come down to dollars and cents. You might find, for example, that a broker may suggest a loan that charges you a point whereas a bank will not—saving you thousands. However, on the flip side, a broker might have access to a loan program that has a lower interest rate and thus saves you tens of thousands over the lifetime of the loan.

Make your choice of a lender based on the best loan terms you can find. Ask questions about expected time frame, points, and extra fees. No two mortgage packages will be the same. Comparison shop just as you would when you buy a car.

But a word of caution about shopping around. Don't agree to pay for any fees up front before you have made a decision on who is getting your loan business. Lenders should not ask you to pay for any costs until you have agreed to apply for their loan program.

It's a Crazy Process Today—What to Expect

As I've been warning you, getting a mortgage has never been more challenging than it is in today's market. You never know where you'll get the best deal for your mortgage these days and you don't know who will say yes, given all that has changed in the mortgage industry.

What will be even more frustrating is that you never get to know how long it will take. In today's market, banks are understaffed and overworked. Loan applications are backed up for weeks, even months. Stricter qualifying requirements will drag your loan approval out to the very last possible day. It can be one of the most frustrating aspects of buying a home today. But the good news is: now that you know what you are in for, you'll be prepared for the worst!

What Lenders Will Ask For—You May Be Surprised

You will probably find that your application experience with two different lending candidates will be tremendously different from each other, and for no good reason. One might demand that you prove X, Y, and Z while the other never asks the same questions or brings up a whole other set of concerns. One bank officer might want to review your tax returns for the past five years, plus copies of checks you've written, while a mortgage broker may not care so much about your past income but picks on your potential future income.

Bottom line: you just never know what you're going to encounter when you start working either with a broker or directly with a bank. Be prepared to answers all their questions and provide whatever documents they ask for. Be honest. Be organized. And be on time if they give you deadlines. A lot of mortgage programs have deadlines attached to them and if you miss them, you miss the deal. Also be prepared to provide letters from your accountants and lawyers if necessary.

A friend of mine actually had his mortgage application refused at one bank because his wife was pregnant, and the bank was afraid of a loss in household income that next year. It seemed like a ridiculous reason for the lender to turn them down, but it happened.

In today's market, you need to approach the mortgage department with a thick skin. Don't get emotional and don't get defensive and don't take it personally. Most lenders place multiple conditions on an application, and they will keep adding conditions until they are satisfied with what they have from you in order to finish processing the loan and approve it. So be prepared to provide additional documents, letters, verifications, and income statements right up to the last minute!

Fees to Look Out For and Compare

That said, here are the fees to ask about and be mindful of when shopping for your mortgage:

■ **Points:** Each "point" is equal to 1 percent of the loan amount. So 2 points on a $100,000 loan costs $2,000. You can use points to "buy down" the interest rate, meaning the more points you pay, the lower the interest rate. Points are also tax deductible, even if the seller pays some or all of the points.

▪ **Origination fee:** Sometimes lenders also call points "origination fees." Keep an eye out for this confusing wording.

▪ **Credit report fee:** You may have to pay for this yourself, though the fee is minimal. Some banks and brokers will go ahead and just cover it themselves and it doesn't hurt to ask.

▪ **Property appraisal:** This can run from $300 to $600 depending on the size of the house. Some banks and brokers will cover this cost; others will ask you to pay for it.

Lots of other fees will arise as well, such as document preparation and courier fees. I'll be going into much more detail about fees and how to negotiate away or reduce many of them when I discuss closings in chapter 15.

 BYB Tip: Don't Move Money Around

Dean Rathbun of Avis Mortgage advises that when you are applying for a mortgage, don't make large transfers of money from one account to another for sixty days prior to applying for your loan. If you have to move money out of one account to another in order to consolidate for your down payment, then do it more than sixty days before applying. Otherwise it can cause huge delays of your loan approval. All of your money must be tracked, so if you have to do it at the last minute, you will need proof of the transfer and then all-new updated account statements.

Beware the Last-Minute Loan Bait and Switch

The bait and switch can happen to the best of us. This is why it is so important to review your documents way ahead of time, the moment they arrive. And also, have it all in writing. If your mortgage broker quotes you a rate over the phone, write it down and then read it back to her. Also ask if there are any points on the loan and then write that down, too.

Even the best of us get stuck if we don't keep close track. I applied for an equity line about two years ago. The mortgage broker called to say no problem, it's all in place. He was going to send someone over to my home with a notary so I could sign all the documents. Well, I had been working with this mortgage broker for years, done many deals with him, and referred many clients to him. So I asked him the loan amount and then reiterated that there should be no points.

A week later his assistant called in a panic and said they had to get the document signed today and needed to rush right over or we would lose the loan. Well, as the document was thrust in front of me to sign, I noticed that the equity loan was for half the amount I was promised and there was a fee of 1 point attached equaling $3,500. I questioned the assistant and was told, "So sorry, yes, this just happened at the last minute. But if you don't agree to this there is no other loan available for you right now."

Had I not been so trusting, I would have asked to have the paperwork sent to me days before to review. So I got stuck there in the eleventh hour. I signed the document, got the loan for only half of what I needed, paid the extra fee, and have never worked with or recommended that mortgage broker again.

Waiting for the Bottom Will Cost You

Snagging a house at the bottom of the market, or so you think, may not always be the best money saver. When home prices are low, I know it's very tempting to wait even longer, in the hopes that prices will decline even further. What most homebuyers don't realize is you have to balance a low price and bottom of the market with a low interest rate. So if interest rates are on the rise but the market is heading a bit lower, waiting another six months for a dropping market to sink lower still may actually cost you in the long run.

For example, if you buy a house for $450,000 with 20 percent down, you will have a $360,000 mortgage. With a low 5 percent interest rate your monthly payment of mortgage, principal, and interest would be $1,932.56. However, if you wait six months in the hopes of getting the same house for $10,000 less at $440,000, thus with a mortgage of $352,000, but the interest rates have climbed to 6 percent, your monthly payment is now $2,110.41—costing you an additional $72,157.82 over the course of the loan.

In a buyer's market, there are more opportunities for negotiations, but taking the plunge and making an offer is an important step. If you find a house you love, put your bid in and negotiate. Once a home is priced to what the current market will bear, buyers will make offers and houses will sell no matter which direction the market is headed. Don't let the house you think is right for you sit while you wait for the market to sink. Another buyer might step in to make an offer. Remember: the bottom of the market does not always coincide with the bottom of your payment.

New Rule: Pay Down Your Mortgage Early

As with any mortgage, while most monthly payments go toward paying off interest, especially in the early years of a loan, eventually you will dig deeper into paying off that principal amount, thereby reducing your overall mortgage balance.

Pay down your mortgage early. You can save so much when you increase payments and pay off your mortgage. The amount you save over time with interest is so far superior to the pittance you can get on the mortgage deduction on your tax returns . . . thus debunking the old idea of having the most mortgage possible to save in tax breaks.

What You Learned in This Chapter

♦ Securing a mortgage in today's market is far more challenging than it has ever been. You'll need to meet higher qualifying standards—more documentation, proof of income, and proof of job security.

♦ Whatever the bank will lend you, say no, thank you, and take 20 percent less. Be smart: borrow less.

♦ Get a 15- or 30-year fixed-rate mortgage when you buy real estate. You want to know from day 1 exactly what your monthly mortgage payment will be on day 10,950! You are protected no matter what interest rates do.

♦ Avoid creative financing loans; short-term teaser loans with big-step-up adjustable rates can spell disaster for a homebuyer in three to five years.

♦ Mortgage brokers have access to multiple banks and many types of loans.

♦ Shop around: get quotes from a mortgage broker and from several individual banks.

♦ Waiting for the bottom of the market can cost you. You have to balance the bottom of the market against existing low interest rates. Waiting for prices to go lower while interest rates are inching higher may be counterproductive.

♦ Don't get caught in a bait and switch; review your loan documents carefully and as often as possible down to the last second before signing.

CHAPTER 15

The Closing Paperwork and How to Save Thousands!

You have opened escrow, or are now under contract. You know your responsibilities, and you know what the seller needs to do. You've had your inspection and best-case scenario—whether the house or condo is old or new, it is in perfect shape with no problems. Second-best-case scenario is that there were a few problems, but the seller is fixing them or you are getting a credit or price reduction as a discount. And then finally, you are on track to securing a mortgage.

Now it's time to buckle down and deal with the boring tedious stuff: the closing paperwork. As you can see from the Buyer's Closing

Checklist below, you have a few items checked off but there are still a lot more tasks to tackle. And tackle you will. You will wrestle them to the ground and trim the closing costs down one by one as you do.

Your Buyer's Closing Checklist

☑ Submit your deposit

☑ The attorney review—if applicable in your state

☑ Schedule inspection

☑ Begin your mortgage search

☑ Review the disclosures and permits

☑ Complete your inspection and negotiate any concessions from the seller

☐ Request and review estimated closing costs statements—first pass

☐ Review and approve the title report

☐ Secure your mortgage

☐ Request estimated closing costs—second pass

☐ Select and secure property insurance

☐ Seller to complete termite and other requested repairs

☐ Prepare and transfer your funds to escrow

☐ Final walk-through

☐ Sign the final closing documents!

How to Save Thousands in Closing Fees

Every transfer of funds and property comes with fees, whether through an escrow company, a settlement company, or a lawyer. Most are valid and necessary, but when you know what to look for, you unearth a handful of what are known in the business as "junk fees" or "garbage fees."

You will save yourself thousands of dollars when buying if you review and analyze each and every fee charged to you. I know this sounds daunting, but it's not.

I discovered many of the following money-saving tips and simple explanations of extremely complicated processes through trial and error. The rest I learned from the pros. But now you get them all in one place—and they will save you hours of stress and lots of money.

The closing process is full of legal language and very specific terminology. It can be intimidating, to say the least. The greatest lesson I can teach you is that if you don't understand a term or a process, *just ask*. I do it all the time. Make it your business to find out why things are done in a certain manner and why they are charging you so much to do it.

What Is the Estimated Closing Costs Statement?

Almost everything you will have to pay for is going to be listed in the *estimated closing costs statement*. Technically known as the "HUD-1 settlement statement" closing form, this is issued to you just prior to closing. It was created to make it easy to review closing costs. By law, it lists all of the closing costs associated with your transaction. It includes all of the one-time closing costs, such as title transfer charges, Realtor commissions, recording fees, etc. It also includes an estimate of "recurring fees," such as your first month's mortgage payment, your first payment toward property taxes, your first six months to one year of homeowner's insurance, and so on. It's all there.

The Insider Secret to Unlocking the Estimated Closing Costs Statement

It's *essential* that you request and carefully review your estimated closing costs statement. You are not going to settle for the customary *one* estimated closing costs statement. You are going to request a total of *three* along the way: at the *beginning* of escrow, *during* escrow, and *right before* closing. This gives you a chance to review all the charges and credits throughout the escrow period and have opportunities to negotiate them.

Request and Review the Estimated Closing Costs Statement Three Times

1. **Right after you open escrow or go under contract,** ask for a preliminary estimated closing costs statement. This gives you a basic idea up front of what fees you have to pay. You can start to question which ones are valid and which ones are junk. These first estimated closing costs will be just that—very estimated. The escrow officer or lawyer will not yet know what many of the fees, such as mortgage fees and title fees, will be yet, but it still gives you an overall idea and a starting point.
2. **After the inspection and confirmation of your mortgage approval,** ask for an updated version. You'll see a much more accurate calculation of the funds you are going to need to close, as well as any suspicious fees or items you believe may be negotiable.
3. **A few days before closing,** request the final estimated closing costs statement. Review it immediately! Keep time on your side. Do not wait until the day before closing to question fees. All parties involved will be scrambling to tie up loose ends and will not have the time to give you the service and the concessions you need.

 BYB Buyer's Blunder: Waiting Till the Last Minute to Review Documents

One of the big mistakes buyers make is that they don't read every document thoroughly and ask questions as soon as they review the paperwork. They can head off problems, catch mistakes and overcharges, and save time and a lot of money if they would immediately check documents and respond quickly. As soon as they are sent to you, read them. Don't let them pile up on your desk.

BYB Tip: Stay Calm

Don't get crazy when you first review your estimated closing costs statement. Escrow companies intentionally estimate high to make sure they are in the black at closing. But start questioning immediately to get costs reduced.

Buyer's Estimated Closing Costs Statement

To give you an idea of what to expect, here is an actual estimated closing costs statement from a house purchased for $631,500.

PROPERTY: 123 Dreamhouse Lane	DATE: March 8, 2005
BUYER: James Pelk	CLOSING DATE: March 17, 2005
	ESCROW NO.: 02-701560-S8
FINANCIAL CONSIDERATION	**DEBITS** **CREDITS**
Total Consideration	631,500.00
Deposit	18,300.00
Deposit Credit	845.00
New 1st Trust Deed	505,200.00
LOAN INFORMATION **(Charges $2,296.79)**	
Appraisal Fee	275.00
Credit Report	24.66
Tax Service	79.00
Processing Fee	395.00
Underwriting Fee	400.00
Flood Cert.	18.00
Interest at 5.6250% from 03/17/2005 to 04/01/2005	1,105.13

PRORATIONS AND ADJUSTMENTS	
Taxes at $524 10/semi-annually from 03/17/2005 to 07/01/2005	302.81
OTHER DEBITS/CREDITS	
Estimate Insurance	1,566.12
Estimate Messenger	70.00
Estimate Wire	25.00
Estimate Notary	80.00
TITLE/TAXES/RECORDING CHARGES	
ALTA Loan Policy Fee $506K	640.00
Policy Endorsements to Title Ins. Co.	200.00
Sub Escrow Fee to Title Ins. Co.	65.00
ALTA Inspection Fee to Title Ins. Co.	50.00
Recording Grant Deed	30.00
Recording Trust Deed	150.00
ESCROW CHARGES	
Escrow Fee	1,274.00
Loan Tie-In Fee—1 Loan	250.00
E-mail docs per loan (if applicable)	75.00
Refundable Padding	600.00
Funds required	115,029.72
TOTAL	639,174.72

THIS IS AN ESTIMATE ONLY AND FIGURES ARE SUBJECT TO CHANGE

The written estimated closing statement is read and approved by the undersigned and is in compliance with the allocation of costs in the Residential Purchase Agreement and Joint Escrow Instructions and/or subsequent instructions in the above numbered escrow.

James Pelk, Homebuyer

Junk Fees: Ones to Look For—and Get Rid Of

It must be reiterated: Be vigilant! Although your eyes are glazing over as you examine all those statements, be strong about questioning every listed fee. In some cases you can point your finger at your seller, lender, or escrow company. Also, ask questions to make sure the closing company hasn't mistakenly added any sellers' fees to your side of the form as well.

"If it walks like a duck and quacks like a duck, it's a duck!" Well, some fees are not all they are quacked up to be. They are junk. If you see the ones listed below, scrutinize them and *ask* if they are necessary or negotiable.

Mortgage Loan Fees

- **Application fee**—This can sometimes be reduced or removed.

- **Assumption fee**—This can be too high.

- **Courier fee**—Was a courier ever used and is this necessary? Ask for details.

- **Points**—Are they what you agreed to?

- **Lender's attorney's fee**—Ask to have this removed.

- **Lender's title insurance**—This can often be too high.

- **Extra costs for appraiser's photography**—This is just silly.

- **Fee to receive a copy of your loan schedule printout**—Ask to have this waived.

- **Origination fee**—Usually another name for loan points.

- **Download document fees**—These can often be waived.

Title Fees

- **Document preparation fee**—This is often too high.

- **Escrow charges**—These can often be too high.

- **Impound setup**—This is an extra fee.

- **Loan tie-in fee**—Try to negotiate this away.

- **Underwriting review fee**—Try to get this waived.

- **Warehousing fee**—This is a junk fee that covers the cost of storing your documents. Get it removed.

- **Writing and managing documents fees**—Ask to have these removed.

- **Sub-escrow fee**—Ask to have this waived.

Miscellaneous

- **Realtor commission**—Make sure it's accurate.

- **Closing review fee**—Ask to have this waived.

- **Document drawing/signing fee**—This is often too high.

- **Padding**—This should come back to you and is only used as backup money.

Paying the Lawyer

How much is a reasonable amount to pay for a lawyer? Wow, that is a tough one. Lawyers' hourly fees can range anywhere from $175 to $500 an hour, or more, depending on your location and how willing you are to hire a big firm or an individual lawyer. I always prefer to ask for a flat fee payment. That way you know what you are going to pay right from the get-go. On average a lawyer could charge around $1,000 to do the entire process. Of course, if things get tricky or difficult and problems arise with the seller, your lawyer fees may go up. But if that happens, make sure to ask right away, "How much more is that going to cost me?" And also keep in mind that new and preconstruction closings can and often do drag on for months, costing you more in lawyer fees.

More Closing Paperwork—Title, Appraisal, Insurance

Title, Title, Title

Many items and terms thrown around when purchasing a house have the word "title" in them. It's just downright confusing. But you have to know what all these "titles" mean, do, and stand for. They are all important—some more than others—some cost you money and, fortunately for you, some cost the seller money. So I think the best way to address them all is to go down the list in the order in which you will encounter them as you work through the buying process:

1. Taking title

2. Title company

3. Title search—title report

4. Clear title

5. Title insurance

Taking the Title

Who is going to take title to this house? In non-"title" terms, that is asking: Who is actually going to own this house? Make sense? How you "take title" is actually just the name of the person, persons, or entity that will own the house, and in what form. Here are five ways you can "take title":

- You can actually hold title in your own name.

- Joint tenancy allows you to hold it with another person who has rights of survivorship. Generally this is used in marriages as there is an equal share of ownership and rights of survivorship.

- You can hold it with another person, which is called tenants in common. Under this arrangement, the share doesn't have to be equal and the interest may be passed to remaining owners or to others.

- You can hold title in a partnership, limited liability company, corporation, or trust.

- You can hold title with a legal spouse, which is called tenancy by entirety.

Taking Title with a Same-Sex Partner, a Friend, or a Relative

I am often asked to advise same-sex couples on the topic of homeownership. I think this is because there is so much uncertainty about the current legal policies and specific rights for gay and lesbian couples holding title together on their homes. Regardless of whether or not you're in a state that legally recognizes same-sex marriages, you need to protect your interests in the house you are about to purchase. Thus, in addition to taking title together either as tenants in common or under joint tenancy, you need to have an additional agreement.

For any couples who have yet to walk down the aisle, or who are not legally allowed to marry yet, it's important to draw up a contract with a real estate attorney before closing. Let's face it: as with traditional marriages, relationships, and friendships, compatibility with family members can often go terribly wrong. It's important to have a written agreement right from the very beginning that outlines the issues of who pays what. You need to define:

- What percentage of the mortgage is paid by each person.

- What percentage of the maintenance is paid by each person.

- Exactly what each person is entitled to if one person wants out of the property and the other one doesn't.

- And of course, how assets will be divided in the event of a split.

Nobody likes to talk about this stuff up front, but it's better to discuss these issues while everyone is lovey-dovey than to try to negotiate them later after things have turned ugly. So, with your lover, friends, and family . . . lay it all out in writing now.

Title Company

As its name implies, a title company is the entity that handles:

- The title search and the preparation of the title report

- The assignment of "clear title"

- The issuing of the title insurance

Title Search—Title Report

A title search has to be done to make sure that the house and property you are about to buy is clear of liens, back taxes, or any other judgments held against it. The title search attempts to uncover any other people who have any legal right to the property or claim to have ownership besides the seller. It will also attempt to identify any restrictions to the property regarding use or development, such as height restrictions or an easement that could prevent an owner from modifying certain parts of the property.

The title report is the legal document that then presents all the findings of the title search. When it is presented to you during the closing for approval, review it carefully.

Clear Title

When someone asks, "Is there a clear title?" what that person really means is, "Did the *title company* do a *title search* and file a *title report* that shows the house can be sold exclusively to you with no strings attached?" A clear title indicates that a piece of property is owned "free and clear"; there are no liens or legal questions as to ownership of the property.

Title Insurance

Once the title company has issued the title report and designated the property as having a clear title, it will issue title insurance. This is an insurance policy to protect you and lenders against financial loss resulting from undiscovered problems.

When you purchase title insurance, you are basically buying an insurance policy that covers you in case some long-lost relative comes forward and says he still has rights to the property. If he or she can prove it, you will have to pay that individual out. It also covers you in the case of a neighbor who comes forward and claims that the little pathway next to your house actually belongs to him. The title insurance policy will compensate you for financial losses resulting from that conflict.

Unfortunately title insurance is a necessary cost of buying a home. No matter who handles the closing, you must obtain this insurance to help cover any serious problems related to the ownership of the home once you have taken possession.

Before you secure a mortgage, lenders almost always require title insurance. Also keep in mind that you want to have your own title insurance. The lender will want title insurance for his or her company but that only covers the company if there's a problem. It doesn't cover you. It doesn't protect you.

How Much Does Title Insurance Cost?

I personally think title insurance is way too expensive and I am sure I will get some flak for this from title companies, but I would really like to know what percentage of title insurance policy holders have ever even filed and been paid on a claim.

The cost of title insurance varies state to state, and your Realtor should be able to advise you about the average costs in your area, as well as who normally pays for it. You do, however, want to err on the side of caution and ask for more coverage than the bare minimum. It's that old "you get what you pay for" thing. If you obtain a cheap policy, it may not be there to save you in the extremely rare chance that you run into serious troubles later on. So spend wisely.

Appraisal—the Dreaded Appraisal

When it's time for the appraisal, you're at a crucial crossroads in the closing process. Before you can be approved for a mortgage, your house has to be appraised. The mortgage company demands an appraisal because it wants to know the exact value of the home. It needs to know if the price you have agreed to pay for the house is actually what the house is worth. If for some reason you default on the loan, your lender wants to still have a house as an asset that is worth more than the current loan.

Here's the problem in today's market. Appraisals can come in very low or under the actual price that you offer to pay for the house. Why is that? For one, banks are now much more stringent and conservative about the value they place on each home. Before the market meltdown of the past decade you could be pretty well assured that most appraisals would magically come in either over the sales price or exactly at the sales price. Rarely would they come in valuing the home for less than what the buyers had agreed to pay. Now it's a whole new ball game, with appraisers and banks being far more conservative.

Be forewarned: it's very possible that your appraiser may say your house is actually worth less than what you're willing to pay for it. If this is the case, you have four options.

Four Steps to Take if the House Appraises for Less Than the Agreed Sales Price

1. Go back to the seller and try to renegotiate the sales price downward to equal the same price as the appraisal.
2. Offer to pay the bank to conduct a new appraisal done with another appraiser—one who is more familiar with the neighborhood. Maybe even get the seller to kick in some for the cost.
3. Bite the bullet and put more money down so that your loan amount is actually lower. A lower loan amount allows the bank to accept a lower appraisal amount on the house.
4. Finally, walk away. Hopefully you had a contingency put into your sales contract that would allow you to cancel the sale if the appraised value of the property was lower than the actual purchase price.

Insurance: What to Get—What Is Enough?

Virtually all lenders require that you purchase homeowner's insurance. You'll have to show "proof of insurance" prior to closing. Lenders want to know that you're protecting their investment from harm, such as damage caused by fire, water, a tree falling through the roof, and even vandalism.

How much insurance is enough? Your lender will tell you what's the bare minimum required for your particular home purchase, and then it's up to you whether you want to buy extra coverage for the perils that won't be covered under your basic policy. A basic policy will cover things like fire, theft, falling objects, damage from frozen pipes, and sudden and accidental damage from artificially generated current to electrical equipment.

If you're buying a condo or co-op, there are special insurance policies just for you, sometimes referred to as "HO6" policies (as opposed to "HO2" policies for homeowners), and which meet the needs of owning a condo or co-op. This is because the property's common areas, such as the hallways, the roof, a laundry room, etc., are covered separately. Most condo and co-op associations hold the building policies and you just have to get yourself the basic coverage you need to protect your own unit and meet the lender's specific requirements.

How to Select the Right Policy

With the property information in hand—price, square footage, number of stories, year built, etc.—start calling around to insurance brokers or insurance companies that offer homeowner's policies and get quotes. Obtain references from friends, your Realtor, your mortgage broker, your escrow officer, or your lawyer. And don't forget to talk to the insurance agent that carries your current car insurance. As far as coming up with the cash for it, be prepared that you'll pay for an entire year's worth of insurance up front when you close on your house. In subsequent years you'll likely pay monthly or in installments throughout the year.

Make sure that your insurance covers the costs of replacing your home at the time of the problem—not the year you buy it. It's called replacement cost coverage. In other words, if your kitchen goes up in smoke five years from now, replacement cost means your insurance policy will pay for what it costs to replace that kitchen in five years—not just in today's dollars.

Additional Insurance—All about the Hazards

Depending upon where you live, you may have to purchase insurance to cover hazards unique to your area. These include insurance for floods, tornadoes, hurricanes, and earthquakes.

Talk to your long-term neighbors to find out what kinds of insurance they have in place. You will also want to ask them about the history of the neighborhood. Have there been any big local fires that have ever swept through, or any flooding or mudslides from the hills above?

BYB Tip: Order Your Insurance Right Away

Get your insurance lined up and secured as soon as possible. Don't wait until the last minute. Check with an insurance broker to make sure your new home is insurable. Is it in a floodplain or an earth-quake zone? Is there some other existing condition that makes it uninsurable? You need to know. Most lenders require your insur-ance to be in place before they issue the mortgage. Make sure you start this process right away. It also gives you time to shop around and save some money. There are big variations in the pricing of insurance, and you want to have the time to compare.

 BYB Tip: Bundle Your Insurance

Have your insurance broker put your auto and homeowner's policies with the same carrier. You can get a big discount for the double package.

 BYB Tip: Take a Picture for Insurance

Long after all this closing stuff is done, and you have moved into your new home, don't forget that you will have some insurance housekeeping to do. Go around the house, room by room, and pho-tograph everything. If there are some especially valuable items, photograph and list them separately. Print out all your photos and then store them away someplace safe, preferably not *in* the house! In addition, grab a digital video camera, go room by room, and vid-eotape the contents of your home, speaking into the camera about particular features or items that you want to record.

Home Warranties

A home warranty is basically an insurance policy that covers the repair cost of the house's major systems once you have purchased it. I love these and highly recommend that you get one. As we discussed back in chapter 11 on putting the terms of your offer together, you can ask the seller to pay for one year of this coverage. This is a wonderful way of getting some protection from the seller that ensures the systems, appliances, plumbing, and electrical wiring in the house are working and operational.

The policies have some restrictions, and you will have to review their coverage, but overall they are very cost-effective and practical. For example, they cover the cost of repair or replacement of your refrigerator if it breaks down during the coverage period, but it won't cover the ice maker. It will, however, cover all the big stuff—roof, pipes, electrical, appliances, pool, and heating and air. Home warranties only cost about $600 on average for one year of coverage. And they more than pay for themselves the first time the dishwasher breaks down and needs to be replaced.

 BYB Tip: Keep It Up Next Year

I recommend American Home Shield as my favorite. And even after your first year of coverage expires, you can renew it for an additional sum (around $600) for the next year. I have all my repairs on all my properties now covered by these warranties. It saves me a lot of money. Plus, the company has a list of tradesmen ready to come fix your problems usually within twenty-four to forty-eight hours. It's a great way for single homeowners or those homeowners with no fix-it skills to keep their house running problem free.

What You Learned in This Chapter

♦ You can save thousands in closing fees if you review the estimated closing costs statement three times.

♦ How to tell a junk fee from a legitimate expense.

♦ There are five ways to take title on your property, and if you are buying the home with a same-sex partner, a friend, or a family member, you will need additional agreements.

♦ Be prepared if your appraisal doesn't match the value of the house. You still have options.

♦ Make sure to get all the necessary additional insurance for your area; if you need earthquake or flood coverage, buy it.

CHAPTER 16

Closing Day—Congratulations!

You're almost home! Literally. There is a light at the end of the tunnel. Closing day is fast approaching. But it's not time to pick up the keys and the moving boxes just yet. This last phase is crucial. You have already taken care of your inspection, but now you have two more arenas to wrap up. Then, your entire home shopping process will finally pay off when you bring all three arenas together at the same time on closing day. As they say, "It's time to bring it on home!"

The Three Closing Arenas

THE HOUSE INSPECTION   SECURING YOUR MORTGAGE   CLOSING PAPERWORK

Ten Last-Minute Tips for a Smooth Closing

Hopefully, your settlement or escrow process has been moving forward without hitting any major snags. But at this point you need to review these ten last-minute tips for a smooth closing to make sure that you have covered all the bases.

Ten Last-Minute Tips for a Smooth Closing

1. You reviewed your estimated closing twice already and are about to review the document a third and final time right before closing. Don't wait until the last few days or hours.
2. Check with the closing company to make sure the seller has stayed on schedule.
3. If you have negotiated for repairs to be made by the seller, chances are he will wait until the last minute to do them. He will want to make sure all of your contingencies have been met and removed and you are locked into the deal before he spends a single cent on your requested repairs. Make sure you and your Realtor keep tabs on the seller to get them done in time.
4. Hopefully you have been staying on top of your mortgage broker or bank. Have all of your newest bank statements, pay stubs, and records ready just in case there is an eleventh-hour request for yet another document. Make sure your loan is approved and ready to fund in time for the closing.
5. Confirm that the appraisal came in at the appropriate amount and that the official report has been sent to your mortgage company for approval of your loan. Without it, you won't get your loan finalized.
6. Review every document sent to you and return it immediately. Time is of the essence, and you need to be ahead of schedule at all times.
7. If you have had an attorney work with you on this purchase deal, ask him to come to the closing. He will be able to do any last-minute troubleshooting on your behalf. If the escrow officer or closing agent knows your lawyer will be attending, all those little details will probably be taken care of before you arrive.
8. Have your funds ready and transferred to escrow. You handed over your deposit money way back at the start of escrow. But where is the remainder of your funds for your down payment coming from? Are you pulling money out of a money market account, mutual fund, or savings account? Plan ahead by getting the money ready to be transferred or wired into the closing account. Banks, for instance, can often take a day or

two when you request a wire transfer of a large sum. If you plan ahead you'll also avoid paying penalties for withdrawing funds from other investment accounts. This could save you big bucks. The money must be in the escrow account prior to the closing day.

9. Never close on a Friday. Always schedule a closing on a Wednesday or Thursday. Last-minute items often get delayed. Closing on a Wednesday allows for an extra day or two, just in case.

10. Don't plan to take possession of the property on the day of closing. In fact, be flexible for at least two days after the preferred closing date. Things always go wrong, and closings are often delayed.

Final Walk-Through

The final walk-through is the opportunity just before closing for you, your Realtor, the seller's Realtor, and sometimes even the seller, to literally *walk through* the house to make sure that everything is in order and the house is ready to sell. The walk-through is usually scheduled at some time after the removal of all of your contingencies and a day or two before the closing day. And whether you are buying a brand-new home, a condo that has just been completed, or an older/existing home, you want to do your final walk-through as close to the closing as possible.

And don't forget to bring your list of all the items—property or furniture—you negotiated to buy and that are supposed to be part of your purchase.

Six Things You Should Expect at the Walk-Through

1. All requested repairs were completed. If it's new construction, make sure the house construction and all small details are completed.

2. The house has been maintained properly throughout the closing period.

3. The house is in the same good physical condition that it was during the negotiation and the inspection.

4. Any and all appliances that were contracted to be left for you are still in place. If it's new construction, make sure the exact make and model of all appliances promised are there.

5. Any and all pieces of furniture that were contracted to be left for you are still in place.

6. The seller has provided instructions about the use of all systems in the house, such as security alarms, timers, heating and air systems, outdoor lighting, and so on. Verify the location and current schedules for any sprinklers, light timers, pool equipment, or other timed mechanisms.

What to Expect on Closing Day

Whether you live in an area that calls the "big" day the *closing* day or the *settlement* day makes no difference. On closing day you will be asked to sign all documents, either at the escrow office or with a closing agent. The buyer and seller usually do this separately. In some states, if you are "under contract," you may be asked to attend the actual closing, and the buyer and seller will sign the contracts in the presence of their lawyers.

The dance of escrow and your three closing arenas culminate with a flurry of Post-its with little arrows on them, endless initialing, and the occasional inking of thumbs. The escrow officer or attorney executes and delivers the deeds, you sign all the loan documents, and the funds are collected, disbursed, and recorded. It's the big finale.

 BYB Tip: No Checks, Please

Don't arrive at the closing with a personal check for the remainder of your money owed. It may not be accepted. You need to be prepared to have a cashier's check made out to your escrow or closing company or have had your money wired into the closing account a few days ahead.

Taking Possession of Your New Home

As I mentioned earlier, the day you take possession and the day escrow or settlement closes are two separate matters, yet both are key to the entire transaction. Standard real estate contracts generally provide separate provisions for the date of closing and the date of possession. Unless you've negotiated a special move-in date in your agreement, it's common for possession deadlines to strike within a few days of escrow closing. But of course many buyers want to move in as soon as possible, as their loan payments can begin immediately.

If you are really pressed for time and desperate to move in immediately you might think you could simply ask to move in before the close of escrow. How shall I say this? Don't do it! Don't do it! Too many things could happen at the last second to delay or mess up the deal, and then you've moved into a house that could possibly not end up being yours after all.

Technically, you are officially the new owners by 5:00 p.m. the day of the closing and as soon as your funds have been received by the sellers or their bank. The actual possession occurs when the keys are handed over to the new owners. Even if you're ready to grab the keys and the garage door opener and race over to the house with your caravan of movers on the day of the closing, you should wait until the deed is recorded, making the change of ownership official. This usually happens the next business day.

Here's my advice: be very clear about when you plan to take possession before arriving for the final closing. If your ideal move-in date was never discussed during your negotiations, you need to come to an agreement with your sellers before you make a move.

Delivering the Property

Delivering the property is an important issue. Just because your sellers have sold the property doesn't mean they should just hand over the keys and yell "good luck" as they drive away with a check in their hands. There are a few more things you are going to want handed over to you at the closing.

Final Buyer's Delivery Checklist

❏ The keys

❏ The garage door openers

❏ The alarm codes

❏ All the warranties and instruction booklets for all appliances, built-ins, etc.

❏ The day trash is picked up

❏ The contact info for:

   ❏ Gardener

   ❏ Utility companies

   ❏ Cable or digital satellite provider

   ❏ Garage door company

   ❏ Roofing company

   ❏ Tradesman and contractor who have done work on the house

---

 BYB Tip: Moving In, Moving On

One thing I'd like to remind you here: For you first time homebuyers, don't forget to let your landlord know you're moving. If you're currently a renter, then you need to think about giving your landlord notice around the time you open escrow or, better yet, around the time when you have secured your mortgage. Most people need to give their landlord thirty or sometimes sixty days notice. You don't want to end up paying rent and mortgage at the same time.

Congratulations! It's All Yours!

You did it. You bought a house that is now going to become your home. Maybe you're a first-time homebuyer, or maybe you have just traded up, traded down, or just needed to move. Hopefully with the help of this book, it has been a relatively painless, and dare I say pleasant, experience.

*   *   *

My goal in writing this book has been to create a house-buying road map for today's market. I have seen so many homebuyers jump into the market ill prepared and uninformed. And without this information in hand, buying a home is a little bit like driving on a foggy road. You can't see your destination in the distance because your headlights only illuminate the first one hundred feet in front of you. So you blindly hope that if you keep driving the hundred feet and then the next hundred feet and then the next, you will ultimately reach your destination or goal.

This book, I hope, has lifted that fog and allowed you to see the entire home-buying process from start to finish. Beginning from mile marker one to your goal many miles down the road.

Today's market presents so many new challenges for homebuyers as well as new rules and guidelines. There is no one out there explaining the *right* way to buy a home today. The safe way. The smart way. Until now.

You are no longer a novice homebuyer, with little knowledge or understanding of the process. You now know what to expect, and when to expect it. You now know how to judge your own financial limitations and are equipped with lots of tools to honestly evaluate how much house you can afford. You now know many of the potholes, the land mines, and the costliest mistakes—and how to avoid them.

What am I trying to say here? You are officially an empowered, educated, and smart homebuyer.

Congratulations!

Appendix: Internet Resource Guide

www.MichaelCorbett.com: My Web site

House Shopping Internet Sites

www.cyberhomes.com
www.foreclosures.com
www.home-listings.org
www.homeloans.va.gov
www.homepages.com
www.homepath.com
www.homeroute.com
www.homes.com
www.homesales.gov
www.homesdatabase.com
www.homeseekers.com
www.homesteps.com
www.househunt.com
www.hud.gov
www.mls.com
www.propertyshark.com
www.real-estate.com
www.realestate.com
www.realestatebook.com

www.reals.com
www.realtor.com
www.realtytrac.com
www.trulia.com
www.zillow.com

Other Helpful Sites

www.ahs.com: American Home Shield, a home warranty site

www.angieslist.com: Angie's List, a resource for tradesmen, contractors, and repairs

www.ashi.org: American Society of Home Inspectors

www.closings.com: Closing and escrow information

www.coldwellbanker.com: Coldwell Banker Real Estate

www.coldwellbanker.com/BeforeYouBuy: *Before You Buy!* official site

www.equifax.com: Personal credit site

www.experian.com: Personal credit site

www.extratv.com: NBC's *Extra*

www.fhfa.gov: Federal Housing Finance Agency

www.finishrich.com: David Bach's official site

www.foundationsllc.com: Resource for designing, building, renovating

www.ftc.gov: The Federal Trade Commission

www.learningannex.com: Resource for real estate how-to classes

www.lowes.com: One-stop home improvement store
  www.lowescreativeideas.com
  www.lowes.com/home101

www.martindale.com: Directory of attorneys

www.mortgage.com: Online mortgage resource

www.myfico.com: Featuring Suze Orman's FICO-improving kits

www.oneminuteU.com: Online classes and lectures on real estate topics

www.palmstopines.net: Palm Springs Realtors Rose Marie Laviada's and Bill MacMillan's site

www.suzeorman.com: Financial guru Suze Orman's official site

www.tonyrobbins.com: Motivational guru Tony Robbins's official site

www.transunion.com: Personal credit site

www.thehomeshow.com: National Home Show locations and dates

www.upfrontmortgagebrokers.org: Mortgage broker resource

Index

Also available from
Michael Corbett

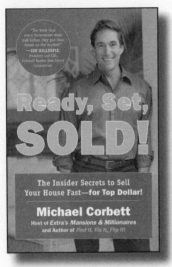

978-0-452-28813-3

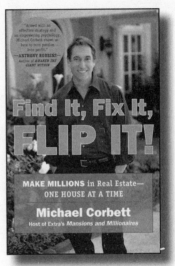

978-0-452-28669-6

Available wherever books are sold.

www.michaelcorbett.com

Plume
A member of Penguin Group (USA) Inc.
www.penguin.com